ACCIDENTS

In North American Climbing 2025

VOLUME 13 | NUMBER 3 | ISSUE 78

American Alpine Club

AMERICAN ALPINE CLUB
GOLDEN, COLORADO

ALPINE CLUB OF CANADA
CANMORE, ALBERTA

LUNA
ROCKY TALKIE
CH 128

CONTENTS

Front Cover: Alex Honnold rappelling off Mt. Hooker in the Wind River Range, Wyoming. Photo by Taylor Shaffer.

Back Cover: SAR team packing bags after responding to a rappel and stranding accident on Cutthroat Peak in the North Cascades (*see page 84*). Photo by Chelan County Mountain Rescue.

ISBN: 979-8-9874576-9-6. Published by the American Alpine Club, 710 Tenth Street, Suite 100, Golden, CO 80401. Printed in South Korea.

FSC www.fsc.org MIX Paper | Supporting responsible forestry FSC® C147056

OR
OUTDOOR
RESEARCH
Rooted.
BORN IN THE ELEMENTS
BUILT ON THE TRAIL

ACCIDENTS IN NORTH AMERICAN CLIMBING

VOLUME 13 | NUMBER 3 | ISSUE 78

American Alpine Club

EDITOR EMERITUS
John E. (Jed) Williamson

EDITOR
Pete Takeda

DESIGN
Randall Levensaler

SENIOR EDITOR
Dave Weber

SKI MOUNTAINEERING EDITOR
Jack Stauss

CONTRIBUTING EDITOR
Aram Attarian (NC)

REGIONAL EDITORS
Daniel Apodaca (NM and AZ); Mark Berenblum (NY); Caleb Bryce (OR); Dan Cousins (New England); Ian Jackson (Banff, Yoho, Kootenay, CAN); Ashton Johnston (western CO); Michelle Leber (UT); Nick Meyers (Mt. Shasta); Jesse McGahey (Yosemite NP); Christine Oken (Denali NP); Christy Rosa (CA); Mathew Trotter (Jasper, CAN); David Weber (North Cascades NP, Mt. Rainier NP, Grand Teton NP); Kim Yee (OR)

ADDITIONAL THANKS

Joshua Corsa, Elizabeth Cromwell, Dallas Glass, John Godino, Valerie Karr, Bill Kinter, Leo Paik, Donovan Smith, Phil Wortmann

AAC EXECUTIVE EDITOR
Dougald MacDonald

Alpine Club of Canada

CANADA EDITOR
Robert Chisnall

BLUE ICE
LIGHT COMPACT MINIMALIST ESSENTIALS FOR MOUNTAIN ADVENTURES

PREFACE

By Pete Takeda

Climbing accidents are a painful yet consistent measure of the state of our sport. Accidents mirror trends in climbing culture, reflect areas of its growth, and follow a shifting demographic. As climbing encompasses a bigger, more varied population, accidents provide external evidence of internal growing pains.

Gyms have introduced many people to climbing and now change our sport with a predictable duality. Youngsters get better so fast that the experiential curve gets neglected. It's breathtaking to watch a newbie climb at a standard that once took many dedicated seasons to achieve. It's also discouraging when, a short time later, they end up in the ER after fumbling a challenge considered rudimentary by most climbers over 40. As I wrote several years ago, it is not their fault, but it has become their problem.

The volume of climbing accidents seems to indicate that our systems aren't coping with the new masses. Arguably, more climbers are having more unpredictable accidents. The big question facing gyms, guides, and outdoor businesses is: How to educate this growing population? The tradition of elders passing down knowledge can't cope with the sheer number of new climbers and a widening generation gap.

Perhaps existing structures can't keep up with the volume of accidents...and perhaps they shouldn't. In the past, climbing was about self-determination and the exercise of free will. The rewards of decisive action were weighed against very real penalties. Despite all that has changed, the consequences remain the same. Gravity still compels us to make weighty choices under physical and mental duress. Whether made deliberately or by default, these choices are in the hands of the individual.

We have the latest how-to videos, iPhones with an SOS function, Garmin inReaches, safety classes, and an annual accidents book, but it's still ultimately on us to measure the risks that accompany every day of climbing. Mishaps do not only strike the unaware but also the prudent, the experienced, and the well prepared.

In this issue of *ANAC*, you'll see a lot of familiar things and maybe something new. I discovered that girth-hitching is fast, easy...and sometimes dangerous. I found out that short falls, whether accidental or deliberate, can be deadly, even when wearing a helmet on a well-protected route. I also discovered that some of my tried-and-true rappel habits are in need of a serious upgrade.

While we're on that subject, take a good look at "Crafty Rappel Techniques" by John Godino—the man behind Alpinesavvy.com. You'll also see what may be a first-of-its-kind article titled "Human Factors Behind Climbing Accidents." To learn more, read on.

Thanks again to our correspondents and to those who sent in their personal stories. A special shout-out goes to all the anonymous SAR members who got up in the middle of the night to help out a fellow climber. Without you, many of the following accidents would have had tragic endings.

Submissions

Share your story and help fellow climbers. Visit *publications.americanalpineclub.org* to file an accident report or email us at *accidents@americanalpineclub.org.*

United WE Climb.
As an AAC member, you're part of the largest Club of climbers in the country—a group of climbers who connect around a shared passion, advocacy for climbers, and educational resources to keep each other safe.
Leverage your membership—and feed your passion for climbing—by applying to our adventure grants, snagging those discounts, planning a trip to one of our iconic lodging facilities, or reading up on your Rescue and Medical Expense Benefit.
Not a member? You're missing out. Learn more about the Club and join or renew at americanalpineclub.org.
American Alpine Club

American Alpine Club | REDPOINT TRAVEL PROTECTION

AAC Rescue Benefit

A step-by-step guide for active members.

Suffered a medical emergency*?

*From an accident while participating in a covered activity?

YES

Do you need help getting to a hospital?

NO

Go get the medical attention you need.

YES

To initiate a medical evacuation call Redpoint ASAP **+1 628-251-1510**

Stay calm, Redpoint will coordinate your safe evacuation to an appropriate medical facility. If you are left with any out-of-pocket emergency medical expenses after your incident, please follow the claims process below.

Can't call Redpoint for a legitimate* reason?

*i.e. You are unconscious and a bystander didn't know to call Redpoint and dialed 911 instead.

Inform Redpoint of your medical situation ASAP.

CLAIMS

Have you just finished paying your out-of-pocket emergency expenses?

NO

Hold tight until you've paid your bills, as Redpoint will only reimburse you, not a third party.

YES

Fill out the appropriate claims paperwork found in your AAC profile.

Claims are typically processed within 30 days, and reimbursement checks can take two weeks to send.

Friends of ANAC

The following people helped make this year's* Accidents in North American Climbing *possible with a gift of $250 or more between January 2024 and May 1, 2025. Thank you!

Jim Bodenhamer
Carla Firey
Eric Green
Richard Hoffman, M.D.
David Landman
and Marian Hawley
Scott Petersen
James Sneeringer
Mark and Karen Stier

Steve Schwortz on *Corrugation Corner* (5.7) at Lover's Leap, California.
AAC Member Daniel Johnson

A climber descending the spectacular Monkey Face at Smith Rock. Rappelling is an integral and hazardous part of the climbing experience. *Joe Peacock—Wikimedia*

KNOW THE ROPES

Crafty Rappel Techniques

BY JOHN GODINO

"Good judgment comes from experience. Experience often comes from surviving bad judgment."—Mark Twain

In my first year of climbing, I almost died rappelling.

My buddy and I had climbed a moderate two-pitch gear route at Smith Rock, Oregon. Getting down meant doing a single-rope rappel to an intermediate bolt anchor and then doing one more rappel to the ground. No problem, we thought.

I went first. I looked down and saw what I thought were the intermediate anchor bolts. They were a bit off to the side, but they looked easy enough to reach. I started rappelling slowly and in control. About halfway down, I began pushing sideways with my feet, tensioning rightward toward the intermediate anchor.

I was about ten feet above the bolts when I glanced down at the tails of my rope. The ends were unknotted and flapping five feet below my brake hand. Not a good place to be.

After an initial wave of panic and nausea, my head cleared. My problem needed an immediate solution. Forcing myself out of adrenaline-induced tunnel vision, I looked around. There, about 20 feet to my left, tucked under a little lip of rock and invisible from above, was a pair of shiny bolts with stainless rappel rings—the actual rappel anchor for my descent.

Grabbing the rope as tightly as I could, I swung left to the bolts and carefully reached up to clip in with my tether. Relief washed over me and I weakly croaked up to my partner, "Off rappel." The rest of the descent was uneventful, but every time I lean off the edge of a cliff on a rappel line, I remind myself that rappelling, as easy as it seems, is a persistent and equal opportunity killer that has plucked many from our ranks, including greats of the past like Toni Kurz, Jim Madsen, Todd Skinner, and more recently, Brad Gobright.

LUCK IS NOT A STRATEGY

Climbing is very unforgiving of stupid mistakes. In the case above, I made a bunch of errors and got lucky.

The following factors led quickly to the critical situation described above, and these are relevant to almost every rappel descent.

- Not having adequate descent beta.
- Not paying attention to the logical place to find the next anchor (i.e., the fall line from the top anchor).
- Not "closing my system." This could have been tying knot(s) in the end(s) of the rope or clipping the knotted end(s) of the rope to my harness.
- Not paying attention to the remaining rope below me.

Yes, I was a relative novice, and in my defense, this was long before stopper knots became standard practice.Still, over the decades extremely experienced climbers have died while rappelling simply because they did not tie stopper knots. Please be smart—gain some knowledge from the poor judgment and close calls of myself and others.

When choosing to knot or not to knot the end of your rappel ropes, our author asks: How many people have died from a knotted rope end getting stuck? *Jeremiah Watt*

RAPPEL TIPS

A few techniques will go a long way to reduce risk while rappelling. Here are a few that apply to a wide number of situations. Some are also not common knowledge.

- Using stopper knots effectively
- The stacked (a.k.a. pre-rigged) rappel
- Improving sketchy anchors

Using stopper knots effectively

Tying knots in the end(s) of your rappel rope(s) is the easiest and most obvious way to close your rope system. This provides an easy way to avoid rappelling off the ends of your rope.

Some people object to tying knots in the rappel strands because they don't want a knot to get stuck. This is rarely an issue. Unless you have unusually deep, rope-eating cracks right below you, the first person down should easily be able to stop, pull the knot out of whatever crack it might be in, and toss it back down the cliff.

A key rule of rappelling is to never go below any rope that's stuck. The first person down should fix any issues and lower the rope properly.

When considering any of these inconveniences, think of it this way: How many people have died from a knotted rope end getting stuck? Compare that to how many people have died from rappelling off the end of the rope?

Case Study (*ANAC 2025; see page 108*): This year, we are reporting a tragic instance of a fatal rappel fall that would have been prevented by using stopper knots on both ends of the rope. A climber was rappelling a 70-meter pitch that he had completed in a light rain. It is assumed he intended to do a three-rappel descent. On his first rappel, a combination of elements led to a miscalculation of the rope lengths in his double-rope rappel. It was discovered that one end of his rope had a stopper knot and the other did not. A stopper knot on both ends would have arrested his fall.

Choosing a stopper knot

The standard stopper knot is the barrel knot.

Relying solely on stopper knots is risky—they may fail under force or pass through certain descenders. Recently, HowNOT2.com measured the force required to pull a stopper knot through an ATC at 6kN.

Tie the stopper using a three-foot section at the end of the rope with plenty of tail. This prevents it from loosening or untying. All knots (not just these) should be tight and evenly dressed.

When the first climber reaches the ground after the final rappel, they should untie the stopper knots—they're no longer needed. If you get in the habit of doing this, you'll never experience the mistake of attempting to pull down your rope with a knot in the end of one strand. (I know this is a common mistake because I've done it several times.)

The Stacked Rappel

The stacked rappel (known by some as a "pre-rigged rappel") is a common technique with guides and clients. It also has some benefits that cross over to recreational climbing. The stacked rappel is very efficient and reduces risk.

Let's talk about multi-pitch rappels, which is where many "rap-off-the-end-of-the-rope" accidents seem to happen.

When doing multiple rappels, many people avoid tying knots in the ends of both strands. Why? Because it's easy to thread one strand through the lower anchor, tie a stopper knot, pull the rope, and let the second strand fall (mostly) down the next pitch. This leaves you with a knot in the "pull" strand, but none in the "falling" strand.

You could pull up half of the rope, tie a second stopper knot, and toss it back down, but that is a bit of a hassle. That's why many people skip it.

Guess what? There's a simple way to mitigate this risk, and it's called the stacked rappel.

As we said above, the stacked rappel is efficient and reduces risk. A stacked rappel means that both partners (assuming a team of two) rig to rappel before either actually rappels. Both climbers will use a sling or tether to extend the rappel device and locking carabiner away from their harness. This extension prevents the climber who remains at the rappel station from getting yanked around when the rope is under tension as the first climber is rappelling.

Three Main Benefits

Risk reduction: Both climbers are pre-rigged so they can check each other's systems for a correct set up. This includes Belay device, Rope, Anchor, Knot, Extension, and Safety backup (BRAKES). It's standard practice to do a partner belay check. With pre-rigged rappels, you can do a partner *BRAKES* check. If we give partners a safety check on the way up before they start climbing, why not do the same on the way down? With the stacked rappel, both climbers can check each other's setup before heading down.

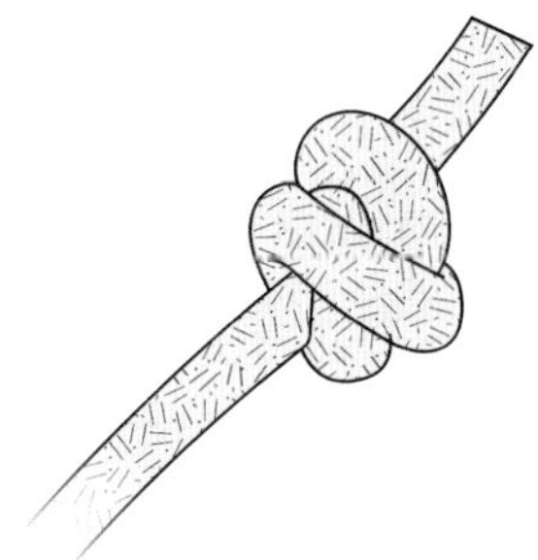

Barrel knot. ***Foster Denney***

Note that this can be especially important if one climber is less experienced. Usually the more experienced person goes first to set up the lower anchor. The second climber will be rigged *and* BRAKE checked before they start down.

Greater efficiency: Stacked rappels are efficient because both climbers set up their rappel devices on the ropes at the same time. It becomes a simple matter of unclipping the tether and rappelling when it's your turn to go down.

On a normal rappel, the second rapper can't get rigged until the first person goes off rappel, thus providing the needed slack. Not so with the stacked rappel. The second person can start down the very moment that the first person goes off rappel. An experienced team will find modest time savings here. But with beginners, especially a larger team, the time savings can be substantial.

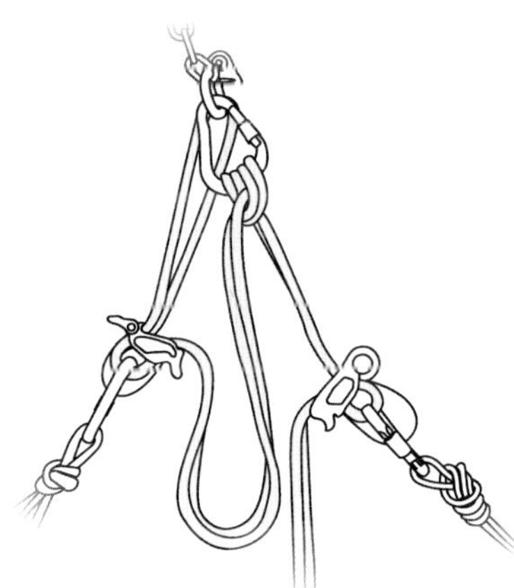

In the stacked rappel, the bottom climber (lower right) rappels first. The locking carabiner is removed after the first climber rappels. ***Foster Denney***

Only one knot needed in the end of the rope: How is having only one knot *safer,* when there are two strands? This might be a little hard to visualize, but bear with me. When you do a stacked rappel, the device of the person at the top anchor has *both* rope strands *locked in place*. This is essentially like having both strands of rope *fixed* while doing a double-rope rappel. If the first person down happened to rappel off the end of one strand of the rope, they would be caught by the knot in the second strand—and because of their pre-rigged partner on top, the rope would not get pulled abruptly through the top anchor.

The Stacked Rappel in Action: Multipitch Rappels

Can you see how this is so helpful for multipitch rappels?

When you, the first climber, reach the lower anchor, you pass one strand of the rope through the anchor and tie a stopper knot in that one strand. When the second climber gets to the lower anchor, that strand gets pulled. The other strand zings through the top anchor and falls beautifully all the way down past you to the next anchor, without a knot in it.

Then you set up a stacked rappel with your partner and head down, with zero risk of rapping off the ends of the rope and without the extra time needed to pull up the other strand, tie a knot in it, and toss it again.

(This may be a bit of a head-scratcher when you first try to visualize it, but if you practice it in a controlled environment, it should make sense.)

Schweeeeet! More efficient rappels with reduced risk—what's not to like?

This anchor in the Wind River Range suffers from many of the issues that can plague a rappel station: UV degradation, rolled aluminum rappel rings, and sling material hidden from view or pinched in blocks. ***Thomas Gilmore***

Improving Sketchy Anchors

It's common to find a mess of cord and webbing on rappel anchors. These anchors often incorporate all manner of stuff: looped/pinched slings, fixed nuts, pitons, and the occasional stuck cam.

Do yourself and everybody else a favor: Cut away everything that's questionable and add new material of your own. This makes the anchor safer, more reliable, and easier to inspect.

Case Study (*ANAC 2023*): In 2022, several rappel accidents caused by aging slings/cords led to three deaths. One climber, using an alpine rappel anchor in the Wind River Range, threaded his rope, sat back to rappel, and almost immediately fell. The cord on the anchor had cut. After bouncing off some ledges, he miraculously stopped after 50 feet. Though he'd done a visual assessment, much of the culprit cord was hidden on the

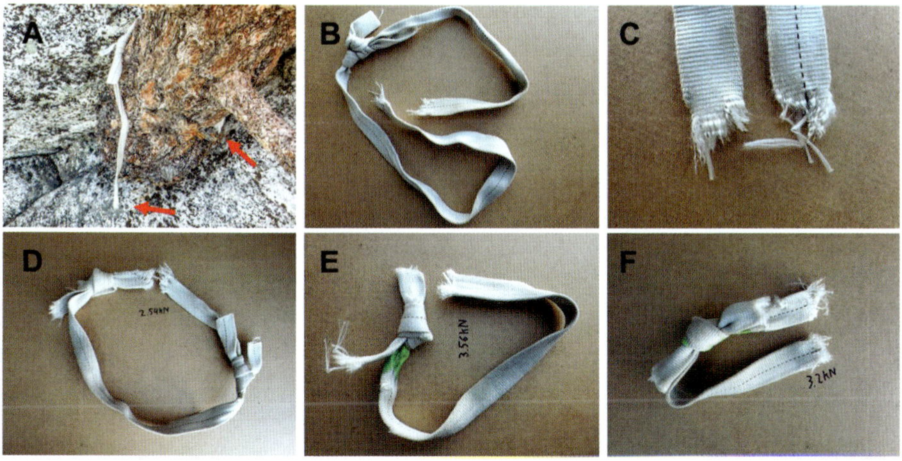

Images of webbing from a failed rappel at Tahquitz Rock. (A) Webbing as it was found on anchor tree with arrows indicating the broken ends. (B) The full length of webbing retrieved with break and (C) close-up of break. (D) Test 1: Webbing broke at 2.54kN. (E) Test 2: Webbing broke at knot at 3.56kN. Image shows the original color (neon green) of the webbing. (F) Test 3: Webbing broke at 3.2kN. ***RMRU***

back side of the anchor block. The severed section likely had been damaged from being pinched by the block's expansion and contraction during freeze-thaw cycles.

Every rappel anchor, especially one that looks like a rat's nest, is guilty until proven innocent. It's much easier to check an anchor that has two or maybe three strands of cord rather than a giant mess, and two or three pieces of fresh cord or webbing are almost always better than five pieces of sun-bleached, rodent-chewed shoelaces.

Here are some good ways to improve a sketchy anchor when you encounter one:

Bring a small knife: A knife easily cuts away rotten slings and cord from an old anchor. You don't need anything fancy—I carry a cheap serrated-edge locking blade from the hardware store that costs five bucks.

Bring some cord: Carrying some extra 6mm cord (15–20 feet) at the bottom of your pack gives you lots of material to improve an anchor. (Such cord costs 40 to 50 cents per foot.) If each partner has this, along with the willingness to cut up the cordelette, that's enough material to improve many anchors. The leave-behind cost of re-rigging a simple yet strong enough rappel anchor is no more Starbucks Iced Caramel Macchiato.

Use cord rather tha webbing: Cord is more resistant to ultraviolet light. It is easier to tie into a secure knot. It's a bit less bulky than webbing so easier to carry and thread through cracks and piton eyes.

Consider the "cheapskate locker": A longtime trick of big-wall climbers is the so-called "cheapskate locker": a standard carabiner with the gate taped closed. Yes, you could rappel directly from the cord, but unless you're building an emergency rappel anchor that you don't expect anyone else to use, adding a metal connection point is better. It will reduce wear—pulling a rappel rope over webbing or cord creates friction, causing the rope to heat up and damage the fibers—bad for the next

The "cheapskate locker" is strong and secure. It makes rappel rope retrieval much easier and gives old carabiners a new home. ***Pete Takeda***

climbers who come along. A carabiner also allows the rope to pull more freely and with less effort. In the case of icy ropes, a metal link may prevent the rope from freezing in place.

You could bring a quick link or a rappel ring, but these have the downsides of being a bit heavy and lack the versatility of a carabiner. Hollow aluminum rappel rings are relatively weak and wear out rapidly. You can always find a spare carabiner. With a bit of tape, you can secure the gate and make an excellent rappel masterpoint.

How bad is that old webbing?

Answer: Pretty bad. Old sun-bleached rappel webbing tested by HowNOT2.com, broke at around 3kN! That's not much more than a body-weight bounce test, which you might generate if you jump around on your rappel.

Sadly, there have been several recent fatalities resulting from this exact situation: old webbing breaking under what appeared to be not much more than body weight (*see page 93*). At Tahquitz Rock in 2022, two climbers used a fixed webbing loop that appeared to be newer than it was. This was because the faded webbing had gotten wet in a thunderstorm, making it seem more supple and darker than when dry. The webbing broke under one climber's body weight, carrying both climbers to their deaths.

IN CONCLUSION

Preventable rappel accidents represent over a dozen of reported incidents from 2024. Unfortunately, they have serious consequences as they almost always take place high above the ground. You'll see several of these analysed in the following pages.

Thanks in part to simple techniques like those described above, I'm still alive and well—and still enjoying the crags of Smith Rock. Living near great climbing allows for plenty of practice. Practice is essential in learning to be safe and efficient with your technical skills. If you're new to all this, in-person instruction from a qualified instructor is strongly recommended.

My last tip is: *Knowledge weighs 0.0 grams. Take as much as you can on your next climb.*

John Godino *lives in Bend, Oregon. He's been a U.S. Forest Service wilderness ranger, a wildland firefighter, and a climbing instructor, and he has an MS in geosciences/cartography. His website Alpinesavvy.com has over 600 articles on intermediate and advanced climbing techniques to reduce risk and climb smarter. The current rappel section includes over 40 advanced rappel tips like the J-loop, dealing with stuck ropes, and the pros (and mostly cons) of simul-rappelling.*

Accidents run through every genre of climbing and represent technical errors, poor choice and/or misuse of gear, deficits in experience level, and more. But behind hundreds of recent accidents lie common themes and recurring patterns. ***Jeremiah Watt***

KNOW THE ROPES

Human Factors Behind Climbing Accidents

BY VALERIE KARR, PH.D.

For 75 years, *Accidents in North American Climbing* (*ANAC*) has compiled and analyzed thousands of climbing accidents, creating a rich source of data for the climbing community. Over several months, two graduate students and I digitized all print *ANACs* dating back to the original publication in 1948.* Using grounded theory analysis—a method of extracting recurring themes from data—I identified key patterns in rock climbing accidents for a subset of the data (*ANACs* 2005–2024).

**Editor's Note: These files are not publicly available, pending completion of research and determination of disposition.*

Climbing is not just a set of technical skills; human nature plays a significant role, which can lead to unnecessary risks. In the simplest of terms, who we are influences how we climb.

Understanding such patterns and the human experience is key to reducing risk and making safer decisions. How climbers act is influenced by many factors, such as gender, age, experience level, and relative position of authority. For example, women are less likely to speak up in mixed-gender settings; younger and newer climbers tend to trust others implicitly; and those with children and/or familial responsibilities may make poor decisions or act in haste due to a time crunch. Several psychological and social dynamics appear repeatedly in accident reports.

The following sections explore recurring themes in climbing accidents, supported by categorized insights and summarized case studies (*full case studies are available at www.americanalpineclub.org*). Each case is followed by a brief analysis and key takeaways to highlight the human factors at play. It is important to note that most climbing accidents don't come down to technical skill—they stem from human psychology. While experience can help buffer some of these tendencies, it can also backfire; overconfidence built on past success is a factor in many accidents.

Encouraging open dialogue about these human factors may help transform painful lessons into collective wisdom that can guide us forward.

WHEN FAMILIARITY LEADS TO VULNERABILITY

Risk Normalization

Over time, climbers can normalize risky behaviors—like skipping backup knots, climbing with inadequate protection, or taking a more risky shortcut on the descent—leading to catastrophic results. Cognitive psychology shows that repeated exposure to a stimulus (e.g., performing a rappel) without negative consequences leads to decreased emotional arousal and lower perceived risk (Geller, 2001).

Case Study (*ANAC 2005*): An experienced sport climber at Barrier Bluffs, Alberta, experienced a rappel failure. This climber had completed hundreds of rappels prior to this accident. At the anchor of a routine climb, he set up a rappel but loaded his belay/rappel device incorrectly and neither tested the system nor used a rappel backup. Assuming all was well—because it always had been—he leaned back on the ropes, became detached, and fell 15 to 20 meters to the ground. The accident resulted in severe injuries.

Takeaway: Don't let experience fool you into skipping checks. The more familiar a task feels, the more likely you are to overlook crucial steps. A process called *risk desensitization* has long been observed in fields like occupation safety (Geller, 2001). While accidents may occur for new climbers due to a lack of technical knowledge, a risk-normalized accident can occur when the experienced climber feels a false sense of comfort and safety. Risk never disappears just because you've done the same thing before. The mountain doesn't care how often you've "gotten away with it."

Gym-to-Crag Transition: Overconfidence in Outdoor Climbing

The growth of indoor climbing gyms has led to an increase in high-performing gym-trained climbers. When they transition to outdoor climbing, they often lack the training, know-how, and experience required to adapt to a new set of hazards and challenges. These include loose rock, placing protection, and variable weather. Because gyms often use the same technical grades as outdoor climbs, indoor climbers may overestimate their readiness—a known cognitive bias identified as the Dunning-Kruger effect (Kruger & Dunning, 1999; Slovic, 1987).

Case Study (*ANAC 2022*): On Anarchy Wall in Clear Creek Canyon in Colorado, a climber who had been "climbing 5.12 in the gym" attempted Power Trip (5.12a) outdoors. He appeared shaky from the start, drifted off route, missed a clip, and took a serious fall, flipping upside down and hitting his head. Although wearing a helmet, he exhibited signs of concussion. The incident underscores how gym ability can lead to overconfidence in unfamiliar, uncontrolled environments. It also reveals how gym climbers often choose an outdoor route based on the grade, although gym grades and outdoor grades often have very little real-life commonalities.

Takeaway: Climbing in a gym only prepares you with a fraction of the skills you need outdoors. The technicalities of footwork, sharp/loose rock, runouts, complex route-finding, and variable protection make outdoor leading a different sport. Consider mentorship or outdoor-specific instruction.

Preparing to rappel after tagging the summit is a critical transition point. *Nate Stephens*

SYSTEM TRANSITIONS: A VULNERABLE PLACE

Transitions: Simple Mistakes, Fatal Consequences

Transitions, particularly at anchor points and when swapping leads/belays or preparing to rappel or lower, are the cause of many severe injuries and fatalities. The most common mistakes are miscommunication between partners, incorrect use of belay/rappel devices, creation of overcomplicated safety systems, improperly tied knots, and failure to maintain a closed system.

Physical and emotional pressure played out over time is a formula for cognitive stress. This is especially true at the end of a long climbing day. ***Jeremiah Watt***

Case Study (*ANAC 2016*): In Vermont at Bat Caves, a climber rappelled with a rope that was too thin for his belay device and did not test the system before unclipping from the anchor. Additionally, no friction hitch or other backup was used. When he initiated the rappel by jumping back, he rapidly lost control and could not stop his descent. This accident was fatal and a classic case of transition error exacerbated by improper equipment use and lack of redundancy.

Takeaway: Even the most experienced climbers can be vulnerable during transitions. They often require the climber(s) to dismantle a system in use and set up a different system. These moments combine distraction, fatigue, and assumption—a perfect storm for human error. Slow down. Communicate clearly and explicitly. Confirm systems out loud before anyone transitions from an anchor, rope, or belay. In a sport where trust is literal, it's safer to confirm than assume.

Backup Failures

Protection: Failing to back up critical single pieces of protection or dubious gear like fixed pins, old bolts, or micronuts/cams is hazardous. Rappelling off a single piece of gear is a very bad idea and for this reason it is seldom ever done. One example of this hazard occurred on May 10, 2025, in the North Cascades (analysis to be published in the 2026 *ANAC*) when three climbers died after a single fixed piton pulled while being used as a rappel anchor. This is a stark reminder that redundant gear is very desirable to ensure climber safety, while the lack of backups in climbing systems are a persistent factor in fatal accidents. Often, a single bolt will be the only piece of gear between oneself and the hospital, but on modern climbs, the bolt and bolt placement is of a high standard/strength.

On Rappel: A stopper knot at each end of your rope is a simple, lifesaving safeguard against rappelling off the ends—yet it's still one of the most common technical omissions cited in accident reports.

Case Study (Multiple Years): Many climbers have died or been injured due to rappel ropes without stopper knots or falling onto a critical single protection placement. For example, in *ANAC 2017*, a 31-year-old climber with moderate experience fell while rappelling from a sport climb after she rappelled off the end of one strand of rope about 25 feet above the ground, resulting in serious injuries, including fractures to both lower legs and a shoulder injury. The incident was caused by a failure to tie stopper knots or otherwise ensure the rope ends were secure.

Takeaway: Protection pulls, anchors blow, and mistakes happen. Back up dubious gear and sketchy single pro placements. Use stopper knots when you rappel (*see Crafty Rappel Techniques, page 14*).

THE PARTNER DYNAMIC: CLIMBING AS A SOCIAL CONTRACT

The Hesitation to Speak Up

When climbing, especially with an unfamiliar and/or more experienced partner, interpersonal dynamics can prevent people from speaking up when they observe a potential hazard. For example, a climber may hesitate to double-check safety systems of their more advanced partner out of fear of seeming inexperienced. This reluctance has contributed to numerous accidents.

Case Study (*ANAC 2020*): A 59-year-old climber at the Red River Gorge fell approximately 130 feet when his tie-in knot failed. The climber regularly used a bowline with a Yosemite finish to tie in; he told his belayer the knot was secure, but she did not check it (and she also was unfamiliar with the knot type). During his third attempt on a 5.12b route that day, he fell from the eighth bolt. The unfinished knot pulled completely through his tie-in points, resulting in a fatal ground fall.

Takeaway: Even experienced climbers can make fatal errors with familiar knots. Always perform a visual and physical check of tie-in knots—no assumptions, no exceptions, regardless of partner experience or routine. Discuss communication with your partner and don't hesitate to speak up—it can save a life. If a pilot and copilot can run through the same checklist every single flight, so can climbers.

The Mentor Trap: Overrelying on the Other's Experience

Climbers often assume that an experienced partner is infallible, but 43 percent of climbing accidents listed in *ANAC* since 1948 were suffered by experienced climbers. Trusting an experienced climber is great for learning, but it can also lead to ignoring personal risk assessments.

Case Study (*ANAC 2018*): While climbing at Echo Cliffs in California, a relatively new lead climber was encouraged by her more experienced partner to take the sharp end. Though hesitant, she agreed, trusting his judgment. During the climb, she noticed significant slack in the rope but chose not to speak up, fearing it might undermine her partner's confidence in her. When she fell, the extra slack dropped 10 her to 12 feet and she impacted a protruding rock, resulting in severe injuries.

Takeaway: Confidence in a mentor should never override one's own risk awareness. Mentees can fall victim to the "halo effect" and overtrust in the perceived expertise of their mentors (Thorndike, 1920; Tversky & Kahneman, 1974). No matter how experienced your partner is, speak up if something doesn't feel right. Trust is important in a climbing partnership, but so is communication. Take ownership of your safety, especially when you sense something's wrong. A healthy dose of self-advocacy can prevent injury.

The end of the day and the descent from a summit are times of great vulnerability. The climber is often mentally and physically fatigued and the decision-making process is often compromised. ***Jeremiah Watt***

FATIGUE, PRESSURE, AND THE DESCENT

Emotional Pressure and Cognitive Strain

Fatigue, ego, and social dynamics impair judgment. Climbing decisions often happen under stress, whether from fear, pride, or peer pressure. Weekend warriors often have great stoke to get out and climb, but the sheer fatigue of fitting an epic climb into busy lives can increase risk. After making many decisions or facing sustained stress, people become less able to self-regulate and more prone to risk-taking or error (Baumeister et al., 1998).

Case Study (*ANAC 2023*): An experienced guide fell while leading a route he felt pressured to complete despite exhaustion and environmental stressors. He missed a clip and decked. The climber "reported having poor quality sleep in the two preceding nights. This, coupled with long program days, high winds, dust, wildfire smoke, and a recent history of illness and family stress, resulted in their psychological and emotional status being less than 100 percent."

Takeaway: Emotional and cognitive strain is invisible yet powerful. Fatigue, stress, and social dynamics subtly erode decision-making. Even expert climbers can ignore signs of exhaustion or risk factors when there is pressure to complete a route—whether from clients, peers, or internalized expectations. Climbing isn't just physical; it's psychological. And when your head isn't in the right space, the risk multiplies.

Decision Fatigue and the Descent

Many climbers get hurt when their focus and energy wane, usually on the descent. This is a hallmark of decision fatigue and cognitive depletion under stress (Baumeister et al., 1998; Kahneman, 2011). Fatigue (physical and mental) and pressure to finish the day and get home can lead to decisions that sacrifice safety. Sometimes, bad decisions are made under the guise of efficiency, but these often are the result of simply being too exhausted to make sound choices. Rappelling errors, poor route-finding on the downclimb, and slipping on exposed terrain account for nearly 30 percent* of serious incidents in some years. **Author's Note: This statistic is calculated from 1951–2023 ANAC historical data.*

Case Study (*ANAC 2022*): In 2021, a very experienced guide (age 35) suffered a ground fall while descending from a single-pitch route in Arizona. The climber clipped into the anchor with a hand-tied daisy chain and mistakenly jammed a knot in a carabiner versus clipping a loop. A busy schedule magnified this subtle yet near-fatal lapse in attention. This guide was also cramming in one last weekend pitch before a two-hour drive home and a three-week outdoor education course. Such transitions are ever more common as professionals, whose free time is relegated to evenings and weekends, attempt to integrate climbing into an already full schedule.

Takeaway: Treat any descent as carefully as the climb. Fatigue and pressure to get off the mountain are often contributing factors in poor decision-making or cutting corners. For example, if in doubt, build a solid rappel anchor instead of attempting a sketchy downclimb. While you may be ready for the day to be over, remember the old mantra of "slow is smooth, smooth is fast." It's safer as well.

UNDERESTIMATING OBJECTIVE HAZARDS

Environmental Hazards: The Underestimated Threat

Environmental factors—falling rock, avalanches, and sudden weather shifts—contribute to a significant number of accidents, especially in alpine and other traditional climbing environments. While these factors are seen by many as uncontrollable "acts of God," climbers can make informed choices that mitigate exposure and risk.

Case Study (*ANAC 2018*): While descending at the base of El Capitan in Yosemite, a pair of climbers was struck by a massive rockfall. They were walking at the base of a route when a section of cliff gave way above Horsetail Fall. Andrew Foster, 32, was fatally struck while shielding his wife, who suffered serious injuries.

Takeaway: While environmental hazards like rockfall can strike without warning, climbers can avoid areas with signs of recent rockfall activity and minimize time at the base of steep, exposed walls. A helmet can help—but only if you're not in the direct line of fire.

Magical Thinking Surrounding Fixed Gear and Camming Devices

Climbers often place a deep trust in fixed gear—nuts wedged in cracks, old slings around horns, pitons, and bolts. These pieces can feel solid and reassuring, especially on popular routes where they've "held before." But time, weather, and repeated use silently degrade even the most bomber-looking placements.

Similarly, many climbers appear to put too much trust in camming devices. In 2023, all 13 reported accidents involving pulled protection were caused by failed cam placements. The apparent ease of placing cams can lead to blind trust in them, even though significant skill and experience are necessary to judge a sound cam placement. Like fast food, cams are fast, easy, and convenient—and, if blindly embraced with little restraint, dangerous and in some cases deadly.

Case Study (*ANAC 2023*): While leading a moderate trad route on the south face of Looking Glass Rock in North Carolina, a climber took a 20-foot fall when his piece of protection—a blue Metolius cam—ripped out of a shallow horizontal. The cam was placed in flaring rock and was not well aligned with the expected fall direction. With ledge exposure below, the fall resulted in a broken ankle and fractured ribs. The climber later admitted he had placed the cam in haste, but should have done so with the time required to place it, "as good as it could be."

Takeaway: Climbing gear is only as safe as its placement and your understanding of how it integrates into your system. When in doubt, build in redundancy—and always climb with the assumption that gear *can* fail. Trust in fixed gear often relies on mental shortcuts or assumptions that bypass critical inspection (Reason, 1990).

Learn the basic principles of passive protection before graduating to using cams. What nuts lack in sex appeal, they make up for in solidity and reliability.

MOVING FORWARD: A CULTURE OF RISK AWARENESS

Many of the most common climbing accidents do not stem from a lack of technical skill, but from well-studied psychological phenomena.

Risk normalization reflects how familiarity can desensitize us to danger (Geller, 2001), while authority gradients and the "halo effect" (Thorndike, 1920) can suppress vital safety communication. Decision fatigue (Baumeister et al., 1998) undermines judgment during long or stressful climbs, and trust in fixed gear often relies on heuristics that bypass critical inspection (Reason, 1990). This analysis

A culture of awareness promotes learning, understanding, and mindfulness. This includes climbing.
Dawn Kish

draws from grounded theory and accident data, but the patterns echo decades of human factors research from fields like aviation, health care, and behavioral economics. By recognizing these recurring themes, we, as climbers, can actively manage risk and ensure what we all want: a day filled with stoke and climbing in the great outdoors.

My training in social science research as a means to understanding human behavior may provide a new lens to learn from the lived experience of others and to prevent future accidents. It is a privilege to be able to review accidents after the fact, and by no means does this research intend to lay blame or responsibility at the feet of those impacted. My hope is for this work to foster conversations within the climbing community about what we have to learn from these accidents and who we are within them, not from a place of judgment but from a place of continual learning, mutual understanding, and mindfulness.

The climbing community is evolving, and increased awareness of these social dynamics can lead to more inclusive, communicative, and ultimately safer climbing partnerships. The best teams are those where every member feels empowered to voice concerns and participate equally, especially in regard to safety. The mountains present inherent danger, but we have the power to learn from others' mistakes and make more informed choices. The lessons in *Accidents in North American Climbing* should serve as guides—not memorials.

***Dr. Valerie Karr** has spent decades studying human behavior in complex environments. She has conducted dozens of large-scale evaluations and research for organizations like the United Nations, World Bank, and USAID—analyzing problems at the intersection of policy and behavior. A passionate climber, she enjoys long multipitch climbs like the Grand Teton, Royal Arches, and the Whitney-Gilman—while balancing life as a single mom with young children.*

Acknowledgement
The author thanks ANAC editor Pete Takeda for his invaluable contributions, editorial eye, and thoughtful technical insights during the analysis and drafting of this piece.

Resources

Baumeister, R.F., Bratslavsky, E., Muraven, M., & Tice, D.M. (1998). Ego depletion: Is the active self a limited resource? Journal of Personality and Social Psychology, 74(5), 1252–1265. https://doi.org/10.1037/0022-3514.74.5.1252

Geller, E.S. (2001). The Psychology of Safety Handbook. CRC Press.

Kahneman, D. (2011). Thinking, Fast and Slow. Farrar, Straus and Giroux.

Kruger, J., & Dunning, D. (1999). Unskilled and Unaware of it: How difficulties in recognizing one's own incompetence lead to inflated self-assessments. Journal of Personality and Social Psychology, 77(6), 1121–1134. https://doi.org/10.1037/0022-3514.77.6.1121

Reason, J. (1990). Human Error. Cambridge University Press.

Slovic, P. (1987). Perception of risk. Science, 236(4799), 280–285. https://doi.org/10.1126/science.3563507

Thorndike, E.L. (1920). A constant error in psychological ratings. Journal of Applied Psychology, 4(1), 25–29. https://doi.org/10.1037/h0071663

Tversky, A., & Kahneman, D. (1974). Judgment under uncertainty: Heuristics and biases. Science, 185(4157), 1124–1131. https://doi.org/10.1126/science.185.4157.1124

Mt. McKinley (20,310 feet). In January 2025, President Trump signed an executive order reversing an Obama-era name change to Denali. While this order applies to the federal designation, the Alaska Historical Commission (responsible for geographic names) and Alaskans in general still call the mountain Denali. The park name remains Denali National Park and Preserve. ***NPS/Ken Conger***

ALASKA

DENALI NATIONAL PARK ACCIDENT SUMMARY

Denali mountaineering rangers and volunteers assessed 34 patients during the 2024 climbing season. Among those, 27 patients were treated by National Park Service (NPS) personnel, and 25 required NPS evacuation. The remaining two were treated and released, and subsequently self-evacuated. The following list summarizes patients treated in 2024:

- ***Traumatic injuries:*** 18 cases (including two head injuries, one multisystem trauma, two extremity fractures, and two knee injuries)
- ***Frostbite:*** nine cases (including several cases of severe/deep frostbite that resulted in amputations)
- ***Medical:*** eight cases (including arterial thrombosis, mesenteric ischemia, Lyme disease, kidney stones, syncope, and minor infections)
- ***High altitude cerebral edema (HACE) and high altitude pulmonary edema (HAPE):*** five cases, plus one case of acute mountain sickness (AMS)
- ***Fatalities:*** three

Some patients had multiple diagnoses, resulting in a higher number of diagnoses than total patients.

Most notable in the 2024 season was the severity of frostbite injuries treated. Frostbite is a preventable injury directly linked to poor decision-making. Climbers often underestimate the extended healing process and life-altering consequences of these injuries. A summit bid is never worth these potential outcomes.

More information on prevention, recognition, and treatment of mountain maladies can be found online. Search: "Denali mountaineering handbook."

HYPOTHERMIA | Exhaustion, High Altitude Illness, Frostbite

Mt. McKinley, West Buttress Route, Summit Ridge

On May 28, at 1 a.m., NPS personnel received an alert from an emergency satellite device requesting evacuation of three climbers who were near the summit of Mt. McKinley. The climbers, all from Malaysia, reported they were hypothermic and too exhausted to safely descend.

They had left base camp (7,200 feet) a week and half earlier. NPS patrols and other climbers noted they made a steady push toward the summit without taking much time for acclimatization. The climbers camped at 16,500 feet for one night and paused only briefly at 17,200-foot camp before pushing to the summit (20,310 feet).

After receiving the emergency text, NPS incident command advised the team that rescue at that elevation and at that time of night was impossible. The climbers were encouraged to continue descending under their own power. One climber (male, 48) of the three managed to get to 17,200-foot camp. He was later evacuated by helicopter for severe frostbite and high altitude illness (HAI). The two remaining team members were only able to descend to 19,600 feet before collapsing due to exhaustion and high altitude illness.

Two guided teams were able to assist the sick climbers. The guides dug a shallow snow shelter and lent the distressed pair some additional clothing layers. The two climbers, who were nonambulatory, spent three nights in the shallow bivouac as high winds and cloud cover prevented rescue. Unfortunately, one of the climbers, Zulkifli Bin Yusof (36), died from exposure and HAI. The remaining climber (male, 47) was rescued, uninjured, in a helicopter basket lift on May 31.

ANALYSIS

This incident highlights some key considerations. First, when presented with good weather, many teams will keep going up without proper acclimatization or adequate rest. This often leads to HAI and exhaustion. In this case, the climbers had enough energy to summit but lacked the adequate reserves to descend safely. As Ed Viesturs famously wrote, "Getting to the top is optional. Getting down is mandatory."

Second, rescue in the mountains, particularly at high altitude, is never assured. These operations present a high degree of risk for both climbers and rescuers. This team's decision to go for the summit put fellow climbers in the agonizing position of having to abandon them in a dire situation at 19,600 feet. Self-care and self-rescue at high elevation are themselves challenging tasks—dragging a sick or injured climber over miles of terrain to a camp is often impossible. Additionally, helicopter rescue at very high altitude is only possible in ideal weather conditions. Even then, it entails extreme risk. *(Source: Denali Mountaineering Rangers.)*

FATAL FALL | Solo Climbing

Mt. McKinley, West Buttress Route, Denali Pass

On May 19, the NPS was contacted by a concerned family member of a Japanese solo climber named T. Hagiwara (mid-40s). He was on the West Buttress Route and was

The 2024 climbing season was marked by calm, clear periods coinciding with very low temperatures. During one of these cold spells, a climber, high on the committing Cassin Ridge—the central rib leading to the summit—suffered a severe/deep and life-altering case of frostbite (see *next page*). *NPS*

last heard from on May 13. Until that date, the climber had been regularly texting via his emergency satellite device.

NPS personnel and private climbers on the mountain confirmed that Hagiwara was last seen on May 15, ascending near Denali Pass. Data later acquired from the emergency satellite device revealed the last transmission location was in the upper Peters Glacier basin. The GPS point was 1,200 feet below Denali Pass on an approximate fall line down the western aspect.

On the morning of May 20, a ground team of NPS rescuers descended to the climber's location and confirmed that Hagiwara was deceased. His body was recovered via helicopter long-line later that afternoon.

ANALYSIS

The slopes leading to Denali Pass have been the site of more than 20 fatal falls. Many of the deceased were solo climbers. This section of the West Buttress climbing route is deceptive. During midseason, the trail often consists of well-packed snow with frequent and fixed protection. The gentle, traversing ascent is not technical climbing. This can lull climbers into a false sense of security. However, the terrain beneath the traverse line steepens, and a slip in this area may result in a fall of more than 1,200 feet. Nearly every year, significant accidents occur on this section of the route.

Solo climbing increases the consequences of a fall. The inability to protect oneself in an unroped climbing or crevasse fall is a primary factor, and climbing alone also eliminates the possibility of a team rescue or notifying rescue services if incapacitated. If this climber had not died from traumatic injuries, he likely would have died from environmental exposure, given the four days that elapsed before the NPS was notified.

In addition, HAI can negatively impact decision-making and physical coordination. Climbing with a partner increases the likelihood of early recognition of HAI, particularly high altitude cerebral edema (HACE), which affects mental status and may not be apparent to the affected climber. *(Source: Denali Mountaineering Rangers.)*

FROSTBITE

Mt. McKinley, Cassin Ridge

On June 4, a 44-year-old male arrived at the 14,200-foot camp medical tent complaining of frostbite. He reported that he had sustained these injuries five days earlier, on the second day of his Cassin Ridge ascent. He had been working on a malfunctioning stove when he noticed that his fingers were white.

At that time, his climbing team did not feel as though they could safely descend. Instead, they continued climbing to the summit ridge. From there, they descended the West Buttress and checked in with NPS personnel at 14,200-foot camp. The injured climber had severe frostbite on eight fingers and all the toes on both feet. The patient was later evacuated by helicopter. Due to the length of time since his extremities began freezing, this patient was not a candidate for thrombolytics (clot-busting medications). He ultimately had most of his fingers and all his toes amputated, a few months after the incident.

ANALYSIS

The 2024 climbing season had several periods of calm, clear weather accompanied by very cold temperatures. Several severe and life-altering cases of frostbite occurred during these periods.

Frostbite is one of the most common injuries seen in the Alaska Range. (Learn about frostbite assessment and treatment in "Essentials: Frostbite," by former Denali mountaineering ranger Dave Weber, in *ANAC 2015*.) It is also completely preventable. Whenever climbing or recreating during periods of extreme cold, use caution and pay attention to cold appendages. Climbers should not tolerate any numbness in extremities—treat this as a problem to stop and fix. Even superficial frostbite can require months of recovery. Severe frostbite is very often a life-changing event. *(Source: Denali Mountaineering Rangers.)*

In April 2024, Robbi Mecus died in a fall while descending The Escalator (4,400 feet, 5.5 AI3) on Mt. Johnson. Her climbing partner survived despite critical injuries. Their line of ascent is marked in red. The route's upper half is hidden from view and marked with a red dashed line. The blue X marks the bergschrund where they came to rest. *NPS*

FATAL CLIMBING FALL | Possible Fixed Protection Failure

Ruth Gorge, Mt. Johnson, The Escalator

On April 25, at 11:30 p.m., an emergency satellite activation reported a climbing fall on The Escalator, a mixed route that climbs the east face of Mt. Johnson in the Ruth Gorge. Another climbing party of two on the route witnessed two climbers fall past them. The reporting party was able to rappel to their location and determined that one climber, 52-year-old Robbi Mecus, was deceased. The other climber, Melissa Orzechowski (30), was only responsive to painful stimuli.

Statements from the reporting climbers and a helicopter reconnaissance of the climbing route concluded that Mecus and Orzechowski had reached the summit ridge and were most likely descending when the fall occurred. The fall was approximately 1,800 feet through mixed snow, ice, and rock terrain at angles between 35° and 55°.

The NPS helicopter was not able to respond until 8 a.m. the following morning (April 26). After a risk assessment and survey of the route, one mountaineering ranger was inserted to the location of the 30-year-old surviving patient via short-haul. She was extracted to a landing spot on the Ruth Glacier and loaded into the helicopter for the flight to Talkeetna. The team rendezvoused with a medical helicopter in town and transferred the patient. Marginal weather prohibited the retrieval of the deceased climber until April 27.

ANALYSIS

It is difficult to conclude exactly what caused this accident. Faded and broken cord was found with the climbers. It is possible this gear was found on route and was being used as a rappel anchor. This cord may have broken and caused the fall, but it is impossible to be certain.

Spring climbing conditions in the Alaska Range may have also contributed to the accident. Climbers can experience a wide range of dynamic conditions at this time of year. The climbers may have encountered vastly different conditions during their descent as compared with their ascent.

It is worth noting that the other team of climbers on the route was instrumental in this rescue response. Through their emergency satellite device, they were able to provide accident details and current conditions to the NPS, as well as patient care to the surviving climber through the night. The reporting party had been in the fall line of the injured climbers, but fortunately they narrowly missed being hit. Climbers should be cognizant of climbing parties above them and always seek to protect themselves from potential overhead hazards. *(Sources: Denali Mountaineering Rangers and Outside Online.)*

**Editor's Note:* While editing *ANAC* in the last few years, I was lucky to work with Robbi, a longtime ranger with New York's Department of Environmental Conservation. She was incredibly helpful with reporting and it was clear that she cared deeply about her co-workers, those she educated, and the climbers she saved. Several times, while researching a complex accident, I'd eventually deduce that it was Robbi who had come to the rescue. I'd have to pry at her to get an admission of this. She is sorely missed.

ARIZONA

BOULDERING FALL | Gap Between Pads

Indoor Gym

I had traveled from out of state to visit a friend, and on February 14 I figured I'd check out the bouldering at a local gym. About an hour into my session, I slid off a slab problem about six to eight feet off the mats. When I landed, my right foot hit the pad and my left foot continued down until it hit the hard floor beneath the pad. My ankle rolled and tore a ligament. I inspected the mats, and there was an uncovered seam where two pieces of foam came together. I could stick my hand down into the gap between the mats.

ANALYSIS

This type of injury has serious long-term financial, vocational, performance, and quality-of-life costs. In May 2025, Fiatal wrote to *ANAC*: "An employee stated I was not the first person to be injured in this way and they recently had funding approved to redo the mats in certain sections of the gym. It's 13 months post-incident and my primary care made me pay for ten months of physical therapy. While I climbed 25 percent of days in 2023 and 2024 leading up to the accident, I have climbed less than one percent of days since then." (*Source: Connor Fiatal.*)

FALL FROM ANCHOR | Unfamiliar Knot

Queen Creek, The Pond

On January 30, Claire Amiel (34) fell while cleaning an anchor on a sport route at the popular Pond area in Queen Creek. The fall from the anchor, resulted in her death.

According to a source that wishes to remain anonymous, Amiel was the less experienced of two climbers. The anonymous source wrote to *ANAC*: "Claire fell from the top of a route while cleaning the anchor. It's rumored she was tied in to an alpine butterfly knot. After clipping the mussy hooks, she weighted the wrong side of the butterfly knot."

Here we see a home gym mat configuration with plenty of gaps that could cause ankle injuries. While padding for a garage climbing wall is a personal choice, commercial gyms should provide gap-free coverage to prevent ankle injuries. For their part, indoor climbers should stay alert for potential hazards at the gym to avoid and/or report them. *Eli Duke—Wikimedia*

ANALYSIS

For most rock climbing, the choice of an alpine butterfly is unusual. John Godino at Alpinesavvy.com wrote to ANAC, "The butterfly is generally not a standard beginner climbing knot. It is almost always used for glacier travel to tie in the middle climber to the middle of a rope. Rock climbers almost always tie into the end of the rope, especially when top-roping in a sport area."

Had Amiel been using a mid-rope alpine butterfly knot—and if she clipped in direct at the anchor temporarily to clean the quickdraws there—it would have created two lengths of slack rope extending from both ends of the knot. Though both sides would appear nearly identical, only one would have been belayed. Amiel may have top roped to the anchor, clipped the unbelayed strand into the mussy hooks, and then fallen to the ground.

Climbers of limited experience or those transitioning from the gym to the outdoors can be especially vulnerable when cleaning anchors. The use of unusual or unfamiliar knots, gear, or systems in critical situations like lowering or cleaning is very dangerous.

Godino adds, "I would love to see more ground-level anchor stations near beginner areas or on the approach trail. This would provide beginner climbers a place to practice clipping and cleaning, before they get on the rock. (*Sources: Anonymous, John Godino, and the Editors.*)

Aerial view of Mt. Shasta (14,179 feet). The Shasta tribe called this symmetric peak: Waka-nunee-Tuki-wuki; the Karuk tribe: Úytaahkoo. ***Ewen Denney—Wikimedia***

CALIFORNIA

SHASTA SEASON SUMMARY

The 2024 climbing season began strong in mid-April, with excellent snow coverage across all major routes. At 7,000 feet, the snowpack measured an impressive 170 inches, attracting skiers and climbers to the upper mountain whenever the weather allowed. Despite generally favorable conditions, late-season winter-like storms brought some spice. Early-season accidents primarily involved climbers ascending during storm conditions, resulting in two separate avalanche incidents and confirming the avalanche risk.

By May, the weather improved significantly, drawing large numbers of recreational climbers. Weekends became particularly crowded, culminating on Memorial Day weekend, one of the busiest weekends of the year. As May progressed, ski conditions deteriorated, prompting a shift in focus to mountaineering, sans skis.

By mid-June, snow had receded from the Bunny Flat parking lot and much of the lower mountain was snow-free. Climbing conditions on the south side began to decline by July, pushing climbers to alternative trailheads such as Clear Creek and North Gate. Summer continued with climbers favoring the north and east sides of Mt. Shasta.

The Clear Creek route remains a popular mid-to-late-season option, especially for novice mountaineers. Generally low slope angles minimize rockfall hazards, though slips, trips, and falls on loose rock have resulted in numerous twisted and broken ankles over the years. Exposure-related injuries have occurred, particularly when climbers become lost in poor weather. While the route is less technical, venturing off course can lead to steep and hazardous terrain.

AVALANCHE

Mt. Shasta, Avalanche Gulch

On May 3 at approximately 10:30 a.m., a solo climber ascending Casaval Ridge ventured off route, traversing onto a south-southeast slope approximately 1,000 vertical feet above Olberman's upper moraine in Avalanche Gulch. The climber triggered a wind slab avalanche on a slope that had been loaded earlier from winds out of the northwest. Injuries included a crampon puncture to the leg and an unconfirmed fracture in the lower leg and/or ankle from trauma sustained while tumbling with crampons.

California Highway Patrol (CHP) and the U.S. Forest Service responded to the incident. Climbing ranger Hayden MacArthur was on patrol on the south side of the mountain, and lead ranger Nick Meyers contacted MacArthur at 10:40 a.m., reporting the injured climber near 11,000 feet in Avalanche Gulch. MacArthur established contact with CHP, and with calm and clear flying conditions, MacArthur was picked up from Bunny Flat and inserted at the patient site.

The patient was found awake, sitting in a semi-upright position, and supported by his pack. Three other climbers and skiers were also present but not affiliated with the individual. The patient was in visible discomfort. A decision was made to evacuate the climber via helicopter to Mercy Medical. The rescue was completed at approximately 1 p.m.

ANALYSIS

This avalanche occurred on the same aspect and elevation as a separate incident six days prior (*see page 117*). Mt. Shasta's spring conditions demand caution and preparation. Whether you're a climber, ski mountaineer, or other backcountry traveler, understanding the snowpack is essential for safety. Before heading out, always check the latest conditions. The U.S. Forest Service and the Mt. Shasta Avalanche Center provide updates on weather, snowpack stability, and climbing conditions. Before climbing, visit the Mt. Shasta Visitor Centers for in-person advice and updates. *(Source: Mt. Shasta Climbing Rangers.)*

ROCKFALL

Mt. Shasta, Avalanche Gulch

On May 26, over the Memorial Day weekend, shortly before 9:15 a.m., a solo male climber (51) descending Avalanche Gulch was struck by a fist-sized rock near 11,500 feet. The rock originated from the Red Banks or Trinity Chutes. The rock impacted the right side of the climber's helmet, penetrating one of the vents. This delivered a laceration and minor skull fracture, in addition to a concussion.

At the time of the incident, climbing ranger Hayden MacArthur was several

Mt. Shasta is a breathtaking and often crowded experience, with a fair share of avalanches and rockfall. ***Jack Dolan***

hundred feet above the individual and witnessed the event. Following impact, the climber fell and slid a hundred feet on a firm snow surface. A climber in a separate group applied a compression bandage to stop the bleeding.

Upon MacArthur's arrival, the patient was mostly alert, but had trouble recalling the event. He also had trouble recalling his spouse's name when requesting she be notified of the accident. Initially the patient felt confident he could descend, but upon getting to his feet, he could not support his weight. While the patient remained alert, his overall energy level and mental stamina were decreasing, and he developed a severe headache and nausea.

Given the symptoms of possible traumatic brain injury (TBI) and the favorable flying conditions, a decision was made to evacuate by helicopter. The patient began to show signs of cold-related injury, and insulation and layers were provided. The helicopter arrived at 11 a.m. for delivery to Mercy Medical Center.

ANALYSIS

This climber was prudent to wear a helmet; however, as we see in this case, a helmet can't always protect against a fast-moving rock. Avalanche Gulch has the highest exposure to rockfall on Mt. Shasta, but one can minimize the risk by climbing earlier in the season and early in the day. *(Source: Mt. Shasta Climbing Rangers.)*

HYPOTHERMIA

Mt. Shasta, Avalanche Gulch

On June 2, an early-to-mid-20s climber descending Avalanche Gulch returned to Helen Lake (10,400 feet) with symptoms of mild hypothermia. Climbing rangers Eric Falconer and Hayden MacArthur were notified of the individual's condition by his two climbing partners and responded to provide support. Primary symptoms included shivering and intense physical and mental discomfort. Temperatures had been cold on the upper mountain, with strong wind out of the west and intermittent rain.

The soaking wet climber was found in his tent and sleeping bag at Helen Lake, still in his wet layers. These were removed and he was bundled with dry sleeping bags. Minor abrasions sustained from sliding on firm snow surfaces were bandaged. Hot-water bottles were inserted into his sleeping bag, and the climber was encouraged to eat and drink. Rangers took shifts lying adjacent to the individual as an additional source of heat. Symptoms gradually improved over the course of several hours. The patient and his partners began to descend sometime after 3 p.m. and successfully self-evacuated around 5 p.m.

ANALYSIS

Environmental factors contributing to this case included cold temperatures, strong wind, and intermittent precipitation. Human factors included poor equipment choices and poor general knowledge regarding safe recreation in a mountain environment. The climber lacked a durable hard shell clothing layer, and he chose microspike-style traction devices in place of crampons. The latter decision likely contributed to the slips and falls that saturated his clothing. Other observations included an overall lack of dry clothing to provide insulation and retain body heat. The primary contributing factor to this incident was the lack of adequate trip preparation for the conditions. *(Source: Mt. Shasta Climbing Rangers.)*

LEADER FALL ON ROCK | Climbing in Hiking Boots

South Lake Tahoe, Pie Shop

My name is Mac (13), and on June 4 I was involved in a rescue at Pie Shop. The people on the spot were Steve (71), Angela, my dad, and Dr. Michael. Steve was going to teach Angela about climbing outside.

We got to our climbing spot, and my dad wanted to teach me more about lead belaying using an Ohm (an Edelrid device) because he's so big and fat compared to me. Well, he's not fat, but he's, like, 190 pounds and I'm 100 pounds so the Ohm makes it safer. While I was lowering my dad, we heard a loud thump over on Crepes Corner (5.7), where Steve and Angela were climbing.

At first, we thought it was just a rope falling or maybe a rock, but Steve had fallen. Dr. Michael scrambled up to help. He rappelled with Steve attached to him as my dad did a fireman's belay from the ground. Steve had bloodstains on his hat and face and hands. He looked okay, but he kept repeating himself, so I guess he had a concussion. Because I am a prepared Boy Scout, I actually brought a first aid kit. I can't believe none of these adults brought one.

Steve definitely had a concussion or something because he didn't seem to know what was going on. We decided against walking to the car, so Dr. Michael decided to call 911. When I interviewed him, Steve said:

I had left my climbing shoes in the car but chose not to hike back down to retrieve them. I convinced myself—because of the ease of the climb and having done it multiple times—that I could lead it in hiking shoes. About two-thirds up the 5.7 climb, I slipped off. The next thing I remember I was rappelling down to Lunch Rock with Dr. Michael helping me, since I had difficulties standing. After 911 was called, the Lake Valley Fire Department responded, as well as a CHP helicopter. By then, I recovered enough to walk down with the firemen's assistance, and I was taken to the ER. I was diagnosed with a mild compression fracture on my T1 vertebra, a mild concussion, and some lacerations.

ANALYSIS

No matter how experienced you are, you can still trip up and make mistakes. Adults are more confident than they should be sometimes. I learned that rule number one is to wear your climbing shoes when you are climbing. Rule number two is to be prepared. Bring a first-aid kit so that if someone falls on their face, you have Band-Aids. Rule number three is to speak up even if you are the newbie. *(Source: Mac Miller.)*

FALL FROM ANCHOR | Rope Detached from Open Anchor

Bay Area, Mt. Diablo State Park

I was top-roping a 10a called Two for One (left variation). I reached the anchor and secured myself with a PAS (personal anchor system) to clean the quickdraws. I hadn't seen this type of hardware before, and it was a type that wasn't fully enclosed—a drop-in anchor like mussy hooks. The adjoining link wasn't big enough for me to thread the rope, so I put my rope across the hardware, stood up to unclip my PAS, sat on the rope, and fell. I have no memory of the fall. I blacked out and woke up in a hospital operating room.

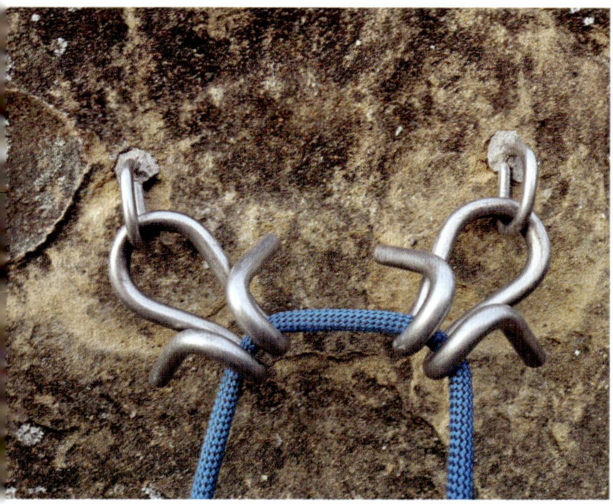

This ram's horn anchor on a route called Two for One in Mt. Diablo State Park was involved in a near-fatal accident in October. It is possible the climber did not set the rope in the lowest and most secure position in the horns before she attempted to lower. *Sean Burke/Kim Harrison*

I broke my left ulna, two ribs on my right ribcage, part of a vertebra, my sacrum, and the ball joint on top of a femur. My helmet broke, and there was a small gash on the left side of my head. I also hit my left butt cheek; the nerve endings have no feeling in that area. I had one surgery to cut off part of the fractured vertebra and to drain a hematoma. I was hospitalized for four days.

ANALYSIS

My climbing friends and I determined that it was ram's horns that I encountered at the anchor. I hadn't wiggled the rope underneath the curled part of the horns that would have prevented the rope from slipping out. Either that or, when I unclipped my PAS, the rope came out. I fell 30 feet and rolled at least ten feet more downhill, along with the rope. It happened quickly, and K (my friend) didn't see what happened at the anchor, because my body blocked her view. K ran to get cell reception and called 911. *(Sources: Jenna Chan, Bay Area Climbers Coalition, and the Editors.)*

**Editor's Note:* Confusion can exist on how to use any unfamiliar fixed hardware. The ram's horn is an open fixture, similar to mussy hooks but much less common in the United States. While there's an advantage in having fewer necessary steps before lowering (including untying and retying), ram's horns are inherently less secure than closed anchors. Two fatalities occurred in Austria—Peilstein (2022) and Martinswand (ca 2020)—in which climbers died when the rope became detached from ram's horns while rappelling. This accident illustrates the peril when anchor hardware attempts to balance convenience and safety. That said, no anchor is foolproof, and no design can negate human error.

This photo of Tenaya Peak shows a section of the descent (red line). The end of the red line marks where an unroped climber slipped and fell. The yellow arrowed X shows where the 70-foot fall ended. *Russell Bangert*

LONG FALL ON SLAB | Descending Unroped, Mosquito Swarms

Yosemite National Park, Tuolumne Meadows, Tenaya Peak

On June 13, my longtime partner Samuel Schaefer (30) and I, Russell Bangert (37), were enjoying the Northwest Buttress of Tenaya Peak (1,400 feet, 5.5). This was my first day in Tuolumne and Sam's third time up the route. As we finished the climb, storms were building in the distance. We quickly scurried over the summit and started down the descent...straight into a cloud of the mosquitoes that plague the area in late spring.

The mosquitoes swarmed as lightning struck in the distance. As we got lower, each step through any grass on the ledges kicked up unbelievable clouds of mosquitoes. As I found myself looking down a final section of slab, a premature sense of relief washed over me—I pictured myself waltzing across the slab and then running from the mosquitoes, back to the car.

In my haste, I miscalculated the frictional coefficient of my new approach shoes. Suddenly, my left foot skated ever so slightly. As I stopped cold, my relief turned to horror as I noticed I had walked onto the most polished section of quartz monzonite I'd ever seen.

I turned to face in, dropped to one knee...and started sliding ever so slowly. I fell into a sitting position and began desperately paddling with my hands and feet. I kept sliding, without gaining too much speed, down the first 30 feet of slab. I had time to look up at Sam and say, "Oh no!" I then began picking up speed while screaming, "NO! NO!"

Just before the pitch steepened, I made a futile attempt to catch a shallow cleft. My hands bounced off and I turned facing out, finally able to see what I was in for. The slab steepened to over 70°, and I accelerated down a final 40 feet. I have no memory of impact. The slope at the bottom was steep enough to allow me to continue tumbling another 25 feet as I rag-dolled and bounced twice.

I came to a stop face down on several basketball-sized rocks sticking out of the dirt.

I moved my fingers and toes: "I'm not paralyzed!" I rolled over on my side, moaning. Sam scrambled down to me and noticed I was soaking wet, covered in mud, and gasping. I stood up, and Sam told me to stop moving. I ripped my shirt off, looking for trauma, then sat down and then rolled onto my back. Immediately, a swarm of mosquitoes descended. I picked up my left arm to look at a dozen of them biting me. I made futile attempts to brush them off before giving up as the swarm returned.

We discussed the situation. I told Sam I thought I just had some bulging disks and my ribs hurt. He asked if I wanted him to go get help. I thought of waiting in the clouds of mosquitoes for hours and decided to try walking down to treeline to re-evaluate. I hobbled into the trees and yelled back to Sam that I was going to keep moving. We finished the remaining 680 feet of descent and 1.12 miles back to the car. In the car, I spent the next hour and a half trying to minimize the pain until we got to the Yosemite clinic. There, they loaded me into an ambulance, and a CHP chopper soon gave me a ride to the Fresno trauma center.

ANALYSIS

My best estimate is that I slid 70 feet down the slab, then tumbled another 25 feet down a rocky slope. I was not wearing a helmet at the time. I wore it when we roped up on the route and put it away on the summit. My injuries were a mild compression fracture to my L1 vertebra and a separated rib.

My accident resulted from a combination of factors:

- **Confirmation Bias:** Six seasons on the slabby granite in Little Cottonwood Canyon, Utah, allowed me to feel right at home on my first day in Tuolumne. I walked facing outward down steeper slabs in flip-flops.

- **Complacency in Gear Selection:** I usually carry a small spray pen of DEET in the first-aid kit, but not on this occasion.

- **Complacency in the Final Stages:** We all know a high percentage of accidents happen on the way down. With the end of the exposed scramble in sight, I let my guard down before I should have.

- **Moving with Haste:** The approaching storm and mosquito swarms created a false sense of urgency. These external pressures caused me to rush and fall on very consequential terrain. *(Source: Russell Bangert.)*

**Editor's Note:* Two weeks later on June 26, a different climber (37) was not so fortunate on Tenaya Peak. They fell and were rendered unconscious and spent the night on a ledge before being discovered by another group of climbers. This climber had been using a popular hiking app that provided inaccurate information, while downplaying the technical nature of the route.

ROCKFALL

Yosemite National Park, Yosemite Valley, Lower Cathedral Rock

On October 14, at approximately 5:30 p.m., a climber on the East Buttress of Lower Cathedral (IV 5.10+) was struck on the head by a football-sized rock dislodged by their partner. The climber was bleeding but remained responsive to verbal stimuli. A rescue team was dispatched to treat the injured climber and to raise them to the summit of Lower Cathedral.

The rescue team began their ascent of Gunsight Gully to access Lower Cathedral's summit at 7:14 p.m. On top, the team constructed a lowering system to access and extract the injured climber. NPS paramedics reached the patient and began assessment. The climber's vital signs were within normal limits, though his level of consciousness remained altered throughout the operation. The patient was oriented to name only and complained of head, neck, and back pain. An additional rescuer was lowered to the scene with a litter, and the patient was packaged and secured for raising.

The operation to extract the climber from the ledge commenced at 9:35 p.m., and the technical raise was completed at 12:13 a.m. on October 15. Once on the summit, a portion of the rescue team remained overnight to monitor the patient and prepare for a helicopter operation the following morning. The other rescuers escorted the uninjured team members down to the valley floor.

At approximately 9 a.m., the NPS helicopter short-hauled the injured climber back to El Cap Meadow. The patient was then transferred to a medical helicopter and flown to a hospital for further treatment.

ANALYSIS

Rockfall hazard assessment: This incident highlights the unpredictable danger of rockfall on technical climbing routes. All climbers should wear helmets and remain vigilant in areas where loose rock may be present. This is especially true on long, exposed pitches where protection from falling debris is limited.

Night rescues and team coordination: Due to the time of this incident, helicopter rescue was not an option. Instead, a ground-based team performed the technical rescue in the dark—a complex and potentially hazardous operation. Climbers should be prepared for self-rescue and/or extended delays due to weather, limited daylight, and other factors.

Overnight preparedness: Whether because of unexpected delays on the climb or descent or more extreme situations like a rescue, climbers should carry adequate equipment should an unintended bivouac be necessary. *(Source: Yosemite National Park Climbing Rangers.)*

ROCKFALL | Near Miss, Rock Dislodged on Rappel

Yosemite National Park, Yosemite Valley, Royal Arches

On May 26, my partner and I (male, 20) got stuck behind three extremely slow climbing teams on the last five pitches of Royal Arches (15 pitches, 5.10- or 5.7 A0). We were able to pass one of the teams on the last two pitches, but the next party was unwilling to let us pass. This group spoke little English and didn't have experience outside of a gym class. They were to be first in line for the rappel descent (16 to 18 rappels). It took almost five hours for them to complete the initial nine rappels.

At this point, we decided to speed things up and skip one rappel, so instead of making the tenth rappel, I would lower my partner from rappel number nine and I would downclimb to a large ledge on 4th- or 5th-class terrain. I had downclimbed

Royal Arches takes a remarkably moderate line up the buttress to the left of the massive arch, pictured above. On Memorial Day, crowding on the rappel descent prompted one team to take a shortcut. This instigated rockfall that nearly killed or severely injured several climbers. ***James St. John—Wikimedia***

this section many times before.

My partner got safely to the next anchor and started pulling the rope while I was downclimbing. The rope pulled through the anchor bolts and landed on a ledge, where it got stuck. My partner asked me to help, so I gave the rope a few moderate pulls and it dislodged two rocks, each about the size of a human head. I was about ten feet below the ledge and screamed "ROCK!" repeatedly. I tried to redirect one rock into a gully and away from the party below. This did not work, and I sustained a bruise and laceration on one of my hands. The rocks continued straight for the next anchor ledge, where there were four people standing and one had just started to rappel.

The three English speakers ducked while the two non-English speakers stuck their heads out to see what the commotion was about. The rocks came within three feet of killing those two and about five feet from cutting their rope.

We apologized profusely and offered to buy pizza as we passed them at another rappel station below. We also showed them the location of some hard-to-find anchors. We later bought the English speakers pizza. They told us that the non-English speakers had started climbing at 6 a.m. on that day and eventually decided to bivy around 9:30 p.m. on the ledge where the rockfall occurred.

ANALYSIS

My takeaway is to stick to the standard line while rappelling. Not doing so may cause your rope to fall in places that might be full of loose rock. Be patient. On crowded rappels, it's better to get down safely. If it gets dark, that's why we bring headlamps.

Everyone tells me that this was just bad luck. I feel I should take responsibility, because it was my decision to try and pass. I didn't have the foresight to see the risk of pulling the rappel rope onto off-route terrain. *(Source: Anonymous Climber.)*

**Editor's Note:* Kudos go to this climber who spoke up to take responsibility for this near miss. Crowding on popular routes is a reality and it is hazardous to start up a long route with a complex descent with multiple parties ahead. Consider other climbing options or make an earlier start.

FALL DURING WALK-OFF

Yosemite National Park, Yosemite Valley, Sunnyside Bench

On August 8, at 3:45 p.m., Yosemite dispatch received a 911 call from a distressed individual who stated that one of their climbing partners had fallen off a cliff while descending from Sunnyside Bench. His friends had traversed to the base of the cliff and located his body. At the time, the individual was unresponsive and had evidence of fatal injuries.

His partners initiated cardiopulmonary resuscitation (CPR). Two rescue team members arrived at their location a short time later. On scene, the rangers confirmed the obvious signs of death and CPR was discontinued. The partners were escorted from the scene by rescue personnel once resuscitation efforts were ceased. The SAR team packaged the deceased on a litter through the talus and on to an ambulance.

ANALYSIS

This tragic accident highlights important lessons for all those traveling unroped in consequential terrain. The Sunnyside Bench is an unmaintained descent and ascent route connecting the valley floor to an obvious bench feature hundreds of feet above the ground. Like many routes adjacent to cliff terrain, this route has inherent dangers. *(Source: Yosemite National Park Climbing Rangers.)*

LEADER FALL | Did Not Place Sufficient Protection

Yosemite National Park, Yosemite Valley, Five Open Books

On May 17, at 3:30 p.m., a 32-year-old male fell roughly 30 feet while off route on the fourth pitch of Selaginella (5.8). The climber sustained an ankle injury with visible deformity but no obvious bleeding or loss of circulation, sensation, or motion. The injured climber was nonambulatory and unable to ascend or descend on his own. He called 911 to request a rescue.

A rescue team of 11 National Park Service (NPS) personnel was dispatched. The team hiked the Upper Falls Trail to the top of the route. Upon their arrival, a spotter on the valley floor used a telescope to help the team identify the optimal line for their rope rescue system.

Once the lower and raise system was constructed, one rescuer was lowered to the climber. The patient was assessed, treated, packaged in a litter, and raised out of the technical terrain. At the top of the cliff, the rescue team attached a wheel to the bottom of the litter to carry the patient down to the trailhead, where he was transferred to an ambulance.

ANALYSIS

Place gear often: This climber took a significant fall, and longer falls increase the likelihood of injury. Placing gear more often minimizes fall distance and reduces potential trauma.

Maintain a snug belay: Whenever belaying another climber, it is advised to watch them closely and minimize slack in the system.

Select appropriate climbs: Climbers should be well prepared to climb safely and confidently on their chosen objectives. Guidebooks grade the multipitch Selaginella at 5.8. If the grade of a given climb is challenging, consider climbing easier multipitch routes or practicing on numerous single pitches of the grade in order to prepare.

Study route topos: This accident could likely have been prevented by a thorough study of both the terrain and the topo. Whenever climbing, remain situationally aware and cross-reference the topo when in doubt. A printed copy or digital screenshot of the topo keeps this information easily accessible. *(Source: Yosemite National Park Climbing Rangers.)*

In June, a lowering climber fell 80 feet when his anchor knot came undone. This photo was taken after the accident. The two dangling ends had been integrated in the original "knot." When the climber clipped the resulting loops and began lowering, the ends pulled out, releasing the masterpoint carabiners and rope. ***Anonymous***

ANCHOR FAILURE | Inadequate Knot

Yosemite National Park, Manure Pile Buttress

On June 24, during the United in Yosemite Climbing Festival, a climber led the first pitch of After Six (5.7). At the belay tree, they set up a lowering anchor using a knot on a quad-length sling with two locking carabiners. The climber weighted the rope and lowered. He cleaned the top piece of gear (a camming device). Below, a second cam proved too tight to remove so he unclipped it. The climber continued to lower. At the third piece from the top, the anchor knot failed. The climber fell 80 feet before the belayer caught his fall, when the climber was about five feet above the ground. The climber was lowered and SAR was called. His injuries included a sprained ankle, lacerations on the face, a broken nose, and rope burns on the hands and fingers.

ANALYSIS

The climber was fortunate that he had high protection that stopped him from hitting the ground when the anchor failed and lots of slack was introduced into the belay system.

The anchor sling was found with an intact overhand knot. The belayer, who wishes to remain anonymous, wrote to *ANAC*: "We believe it was an attempted overhand knot but it was actually a slipknot." The still-locked masterpoint carabiners were found clipped to the rope by the fallen climber.

**Editor's Note:* After analysis, it was determined that the climber had attempted to tie an overhand knot but failed to pull the two end strands completely through the knot. He then clipped the two locking carabiners through the unsecured loops. Since there were so many strands of webbing in the mix, it was hard to tell the difference between a fixed loop and a slip loop. When weighted, the slip loops had sufficient friction and compression to hold, if only momentarily, while the ends gradually crept toward release. *(Sources: Anonymous and ANAC Canada Editor Robert Chisnall.)*

FALL WHILE SCRAMBLING

Sierra Nevada, Mt. Whitney

Ian Fried (33) and I (Tobias Tillemans, 46) had set up camp at Iceberg Lake (12,600 feet) at the base of Mt. Whitney. It was 3 p.m. when Ian heard a clattering noise coming from the mountain. A climber informed us that he had just seen a solo climber fall down 2nd- and 3rd-class terrain on the Mountaineers Route (Grade III). The guide from this party suggested that Ian and I respond, while he would find an experienced guide (Dave Stimson, 43) who was nearby.

We packed first-aid supplies, a Garmin inReach, food, water, helmets, a stove, and insulation. We scrambled up talus toward a clearly visible colorful dot in a gully about 600 feet above. At 13,200 feet we found the injured climber. He was breathing, unresponsive, and had an open head injury. He was wearing sneakers, a light jacket, and no helmet.

We took vital signs and found some cracked ribs, but there was no indication of substantial bleeding beyond the initial injuries. The climbing guide we met at camp arrived ten minutes later. Together, we wrapped the head injury while Ian contacted EMS through the inReach. We decided this was not a safe spot because of the steep and loose rock. We needed ropes to lower the patient to a ledge about 20 feet below. We could see a second guide collecting climbing equipment in camp. Twenty minutes after our arrival the patient was still unresponsive. We put him into two sleeping bags as the temperature was slowly dropping.

Dave Stimson arrived with two ropes and a rack. With two more responding climbers we lowered the injured climber onto the ledge at 4:30 p.m. Meanwhile, Ian was in contact with EMS. Helicopter rescue was uncertain, given the few remaining daylight hours, the high altitude, and high winds. We made hot-water bottles to warm the patient, ate food, and stayed hydrated. We were relieved to hear a helicopter around 7 p.m, just as the sun was setting.

A paramedic was lowered with a litter. When we were ready, the helicopter lowered a cable, but it was too windy and dark to safely haul the patient. The helicopter departed.

We scouted a route down to a flat area near camp and set up a series of anchors to lower the litter. Eventually the terrain was flat enough to carry him. It took about three hours to descend the 600 vertical feet to an area where the helicopter could land. The helicopter returned and landed around 1 a.m. We loaded the patient and they took off toward a nearby trauma center.

ANALYSIS

The injured climber was doing the Mountaineers Route in a day, which entails 6,000 feet of elevation gain and a 15-mile round trip. He may have been fatigued and let his guard down after descending the steepest section of the gully. He was 74 years old and traveling alone without a communication device. It is unclear how acclimatized he was, given his origin of Phoenix. He was descending with trekking poles attached to his wrists and doing that is less safe than putting the poles on your back. Considering his injuries, this climber was very lucky to be discovered before dark.

Most rescues present risks to the rescuers. In this case, darkness and having individuals working above and below the litter presented hazards, especially given the presence of large loose blocks. Throughout the rescue we vocalized safety concerns. This greatly reduced risk. *(Sources: Ian Fried and Tobias Tillemans.)*

LEADER FALL | Protection Pulled Out

Joshua Tree National Park, Upper Freeway Wall

In November 2023,* D and M (female, early 30s) were on day three of a visit to Joshua Tree National Park from the U.K. It was D's third trip to the park and M's first time visiting. M had been climbing for ten years, primarily sport climbing (up to 5.12), and was using this trip to get more experience leading trad climbs. D had been climbing for 12 years and was comfortable leading trad routes up to 5.12b.

On the day of the accident, D and M had been climbing routes in the 5.6 to 5.8 range, with M leading and D following to check the former's placements and provide feedback. On all of the previous routes, D had felt that M's placements were solid and safe. Their fifth route of the day was Cakewalk (5.8+) on Upper Freeway Wall. It was both climbers' first time on the route. D led the route, built an anchor, then lowered and left all of his placements in the rock, reinspecting each piece on the way down. The party then pulled the rope and planned for M to lead the route while clipping the preplaced gear for protection.

Roughly a third of the way up, the crux of Cakewalk involves traversing leftward about eight feet. This section crosses a thin, slightly grainy horizontal crack from one vertical crack system to the next. D had protected the traverse with a black Totem Cam—the smallest in the Totem range—placed at the top of the initial vertical crack. M was nervous about the moves. While leading, she removed the cam and replaced it farther to the left in the thin horizontal crack. While doing the traverse, M slipped. The black Totem pulled out, and M fell six to nine feet, flipping upside down and striking the back of her helmet on the wall. The rope had not been running behind her leg, and the flip was possibly caused by the sudden change in force on M when the cam placement failed. No other pieces were pulled out, and the fall was caught on a nut three to five feet below the failed cam placement. The black Totem showed no damage during later inspection.

D lowered M to the ground. M was unconscious, and her helmet was broken. D alerted a nearby climbing party and, with their help, evaluated her injuries. D did not have cell service, but one of the other climbers was able to call 911. While awaiting response, the group kept administering first aid as she regained consciousness. (D was trained in first aid and another climber had a Wilderness First Aid certification.) Rescuers from JOSAR and the Riverside County Sheriff's Department responded. M was hoisted from the scene with a helicopter and transported to the hospital.

ANALYSIS

Wearing a helmet may have saved M's life, as it provided some degree of protection to the back and sides of her head, where the most significant impact forces occurred.

Small cams like the black Totem have more limitations and are more likely to pull out in suboptimal placements than larger cams or passive protection. While it is not uncommon to move a piece closer to crux moves to reduce the length of a fall, the grainy "kitty litter" rock at the traverse may have contributed to the placement failure. When in doubt, place multiple redundant pieces, including passive protection. This will increase the odds of a fall being successfully arrested. For more information, see the 2017 *ANAC* Essentials article on microcams.

Consider carrying a satellite communication device. The Freeway Wall (the location of Cakewalk) is an exception in Joshua Tree because there is a single bar of cell service at the base. If there had not been other climbers nearby, D (whose phone did not have a signal) would have had to leave M and make a fairly involved descent to his car (20 to 30 minutes) and then drive to the Hidden Valley emergency phone (ten more minutes) before being able to call for help.

Being first aid/first certified and carrying a first-aid kit is advisable while climbing. Both D and the other climbers did an excellent job of assessing and stabilizing M while waiting for help. Many climbing accidents can happen in locations that are difficult to access by medical personnel or SAR. In a serious accident like this, knowing basic first aid can significantly increase the odds of survival. *(Source: Joshua Tree National Park Search and Rescue.)*

**Editor's Note:* While this accident occurred in 2023, we chose to include it here because small cams pulling is an issue with novice to professional climbers.

GROUND FALL | Multiple Pieces of Protection Pulled

San Diego, Mission Gorge

On May 18, at about 10:40 a.m., my climbing partner and I prepared to climb Gallwas Crack (5.9) at the Main Wall of Mission Gorge in San Diego. Another friend was with us for his first outdoor climbing session. The three of us had already warmed up.

Access involved scrambling eight feet up to a large, flat ledge, then up and over to another ledge at the base of the route. This ledge was big enough to not worry about falling off, but there was a risk of the belayer getting pulled off if the leader fell before placing any gear. We all wore helmets and were very safety focused.

The ledge was 40 feet above the trail. We built a three-piece gear anchor to secure the belayer (me), and our other friend sat untethered on the large ledge below and left. Gallwas Crack looked challenging, with slippery rock, but my climbing partner had led higher-rated climbs at similar areas, so I thought it would be possible, though perhaps at his limit. There appeared to be plentiful gear placements.

He racked up and we did thorough safety checks. He got up a short 4th-class ramp to a secure stance and put in a 0.5 Camalot, clipped with an alpine draw. He climbed to where his feet were at the level of the first cam and placed another, then climbed

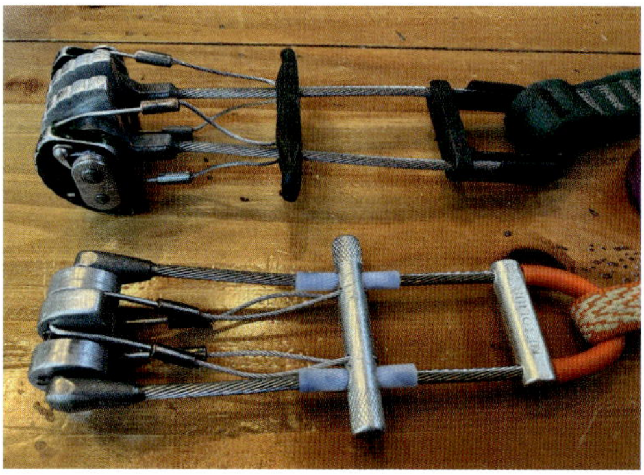

A ground fall occurred on May 18, when two cams pulled (pictured above). Both are over 30 years old. The Metolius TCU is an old version with all cams an equal width. Later, the single middle cam was widened to provide more opposing surface area. The U-stem Black Diamond Camalot Junior is from the mid-1990s. This version's cam lobes were fabricated from very hard 7075-T6 aluminum—a material implicated in several incidents in which the cam lobes tracked out of apparently perfect placements. Both models of gear have been improved over the decades and form the backbone of many standard trad climbing racks. *Anonymous*

to where the second cam was at his waist and placed another cam.

When the third cam was at his waist, he paused to figure out the move, then yelled, "Take! Take! Take!" I pulled in a couple of arm lengths of slack as fast as I could. The rope started becoming taut just before he fell, but it never got completely tight during the fall. I did not get pulled toward the wall as one would expect. The highest (third) piece pulled immediately, and he continued falling. The second piece also pulled as he rotated backward and began falling headfirst. The first piece caught him. I don't remember being pulled by the rope despite the fact that he fell 30 feet total, past the ledge, and ended hanging upside down, about 30 feet above the trail.

He was not moving. Our other friend yelled, "He's bleeding out of his right ear." I can't recall the sequence, but someone yelled if they should call 911. I asked our other friend to attend, since he had emergency medical training. I slowly lowered my partner as he was pulled over to the large ledge. As I was lowering, his body shook for a few seconds. On the flat ledge, he had a pulse and his breathing was heavy. I called 911 at 10:56 a.m. and learned that someone else had already called in.

I clipped my climbing partner into the anchor so I could be freed up to help. I held his head and he'd periodically sit up and moan, then lie back. We tried to keep him down and he would tell us to stop touching him. A woman with emergency medical training came over and did a good job helping us all stay calm. She confirmed that my climbing partner could respond to his name, by turning his head. A helicopter arrived, lowering a paramedic with a radio and litter, who assessed his condition. The paramedic tried to place a neck brace, but my climbing partner refused it. When we got it on, he immediately took it off. Eventually, he was put on a litter and flown to a trauma center. It was less than an hour after he'd started the climb.

One of the pulled pieces was a number 3 (orange) Metolius TCU. The plastic trigger-wire guide on a green (0.75) Camalot was tweaked and was probably the other that pulled. I'm not sure which pulled first. My partner suffered a severe traumatic brain injury, but he made it through surgery and has mostly recovered.

ANALYSIS

What went right: I was anchored, so I couldn't get pulled off the ledge when my partner fell. He was wearing a helmet, which probably saved his life. It's good we had a third person there, because he was able to respond quickly and help save our friend's life. We've been able to talk about what happened and support each other.

Editor's Note: A climber posted on Mountain Project that "two separate near fatal accidents" involving cams pulling out occurred on May 18 (Gallwas Crack) and May 19 on the adjacent Nutcracker (5.9+). He also wrote, "Be aware that cams do not hold well on this rock in hot conditions."

Perhaps Mission Gorge's slick rock, combined with recent rain that generated dirt and silt contributed to the gear pulling. The gear itself may have played a role (*see photo opposite*). Not up for conjecture is that several elements combined to produce an unpredictable accident. The fallen leader was 34 years old and had "many years" of trad experience. The cams did not suffer obvious deformation that would have indicated a high load. As the belayer stated, "They just came right out, with seemingly less than body weight. They didn't slow the fall at all." (*Sources: Anonymous and MountainProject.com.*)

Called by some a "Poor Man's Indian Creek," Escalante Canyon holds more than a few gems when it comes to quality sandstone crack climbs (see below). *BLM—Wikimedia*

COLORADO

ROCKFALL | Loose Rock

Grand Junction Area, Escalante Canyon, Zappa Wall

On December 23, my buddy Blake and I, Chase Smith, were climbing Beside the Pillar (5.10c) toward the end of the day. The route starts off bouldery before going into a nice hand crack. I led the route and noticed a stack of loose, crumbly rock to the left of the anchors. I decided to stay in the crack, though there were big holds on the stacked blocks. I lowered and cleaned my gear.

I pulled the rope for Blake to lead, and we chatted about the cruxy start. I didn't think to bring up the stacked blocks to the left of the anchor. He led up flawlessly. As the belayer I was positioned in a slot with an overhang, so the first 15 feet of the climb were visible, but not the rest. I peeked around and Blake was getting close to the anchors. I tucked back into the belay zone and heard "ROCK, ROCK, ROCK!"

I took up the slack and caught his fall. Rocks were pouring down—small at first, then a microwave-sized block. Hugging the cliff, I yelled up, "Are you good?! Are you okay?" But all I heard was groaning. I kept calling up and then noticed blood coming down the cliff. Some of it fell on me. I slowly lowered Blake, and when I asked how he was, his replies were very foggy. As he got closer, I saw the left side of his face had a major laceration running from his lips along his cheek. It was gnarly, like something out of *The Walking Dead*.

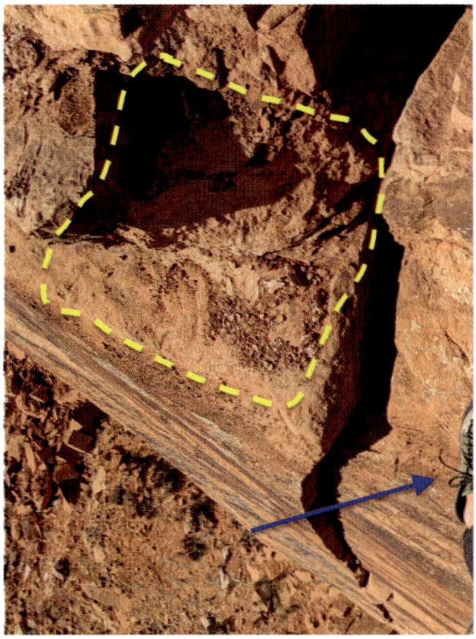

Less frequented than other areas, the routes in Escalante Canyon still hold loose rock. The yellow dashed outline indicates where a huge block was located before being dislodged by a climber. A climber's foot in the margin of the photo (blue arrow) conveys a sense of how big the fallen block was. *Chase Smith*

When Blake got to the ground, I untied the rope and his shoes. I checked for other injuries, but only his face was hurt. By then, he was answering questions and fully conscious. I got his hiking shoes on, gave him my trekking pole, and asked if he was good to start walking down. He said yes, and after I collected some of our stuff, I caught him on the trail. He asked how bad it was. I told him it was pretty bad, but they're good at repairing that kind of thing these days. I also told him that when we get to the truck, don't look in the mirror.

When we got the ER and they saw his face, Blake was quickly rushed to surgery.

ANALYSIS

I went back to the route with a friend the next day to retrieve our rope and gear. It looked like Blake had grabbed the choss pile and fell with it. When the last piece of protection stopped him, the rock was still falling and hit him in the face. I cleaned off the other loose rock and used water and some brushes to scrub off as much blood as I could. Today, Blake's face is all healed up: no missing teeth and just a scar on his cheek.

When I reflect back, the first thing that comes to mind is I should have communicated about the loose stacked blocks before he climbed. We also should have been wearing helmets, as it might have been much worse if a rock had hit his head. The fact that Blake was conscious and able to hike was the difference between self-evacuation and calling a helicopter. We're both Wilderness First Responders and climbing guides, so we acted pretty quickly. I was fortunate to have my med kit and a marker so I could write down details for the hospital. It was good that I wrote down Blake's phone passcode; if he had passed out, I still could have accessed his emergency contact. *(Source: Chase Smith.)*

RAPPEL FAILURE | Munter Hitch Unscrewed a Locking Carabiner

Ouray, Camp Bird Road

On December 10, Jim Clarke (57) and I, Nathan Chaszeyka (45), climbed Bird Brain Boulevard (7 pitches, WI5 M5). While chimneying on pitch six, my belay device came unclipped from my harness. Jim and I finished around 4:45 p.m. It was getting dark. We decided to descend via The Ribbon, which is to the climber's left of Bird Brain. We chose it because there was a likelihood of rope snags on the alternative descent. Our assessment of avalanche danger on the rappels was acceptably low.

Nathan Chaszeyka in the depths of a chimney on Bird Brain Boulevard. Higher on the route, Chaszeyka's belay/rappel device became detached from his harness. This set a chain of events in motion, culminating in a near-fatal fall while on the descent. With the assistance of SAR, the team effected a commendable self-rescue. *Jim Clarke*

In lieu of my lost belay device, the best choices came down to using a carabiner brake or Munter hitch. We discussed this decision. I'd used the Munter many times to rappel, particularly on skinny lines while ski mountaineering. On Bird Brain we had a single strand plus a tagline, and I was concerned about using the unaccustomed carabiner brake system, especially in the dark. The plan was to use a Munter on a large HMS-style locking carabiner. Jim would provide a fireman's belay from below. We decided not to use a prusik backup to allow braking with the parallel strands and avoid introducing twists that would increase the chance of our ropes snagging.

The first rappel went well. Fifty feet into the second, the ropes unclipped themselves from the carabiner. This sent me on an 80-foot free fall down vertical and off-vertical terrain. I thought, "I'm going to die," and my brain screamed back, "DIE FIGHTING!" Because I hadn't released the brake strand, I was able to wrap my arm in the rope and arrest my fall. I stopped just above my partner. There was about 20 or 30 feet left before the end of the rope.

I secured myself with a prusik and reattached my Munter. My headlamp was broken during the fall and dangled by a couple of wires. This meant I no longer had hands-free lighting and would need to point the light by hand. This would become

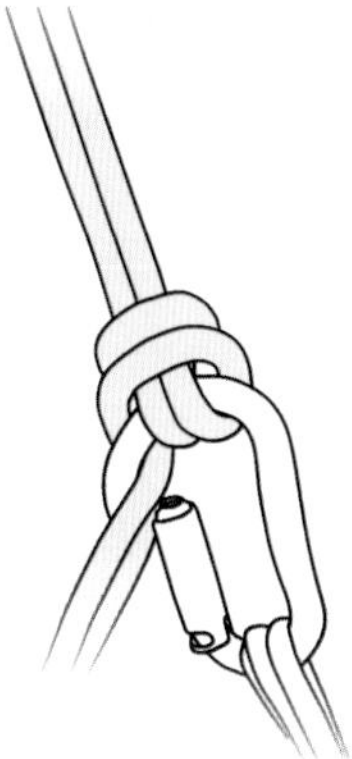

Figure A. The braking side of the rope on a Munter hitch rappel opened the locking carabiner's gate. ***Foster Denney***

time-consuming and frustrating.

Self-assessment revealed that my left ankle was unstable and crunched when weighted. My right ankle/foot was in excruciating pain. There were no immediate indications of injury to other areas. Jim and I talked about a plan. We agreed we needed help but also needed to continue down the rappels, as a technical rescue would take a long time. To get down, he would need to lower me and follow on rappel. The cold was our next big issue. We were wet from climbing, and the temperature was an estimated 7°F.

We were still over 1,000 feet above the ground. As I looked down, I was overwhelmed with fear. I was already quite cold before the accident: How bad were the cold injuries going to be? If our ropes got snagged, would we be stranded and freeze to death? The 911 operator seemed to not understand the situation—did they even activate SAR? I realized that the time for emotion was later and I would need to compartmentalize fear and pain in order to focus on the business at hand. The last thing I wanted was something bad to happen to Jim as a result of my accident.

Figure B. The common complaint about the Munter hitch is that it tends to tangle ropes. The "No Twist Munter" not only negates tangling but also prevents the rope from coming in contact with the locking mechanism. ***Foster Denney***

For eight more rope lengths, Jim lowered me while I navigated with my broken headlamp. As he lowered, I would crawl on hands and knees down the ice and rock. I fought to block the pain and dysfunction in my body. At the anchors, I couldn't use my feet for support. I was fully hanging, knees painfully digging into the snow and rock with my body hanging from slings. The hypothermia set in fairly fast. I was shivering violently and found myself getting tired. My eyes would get heavy, but I knew if I allowed myself to sleep, the outcome could be very bad. I repeated the mantra "die fighting" every time I wanted to rest my head against the ice.

During the final lower, I saw two climbers from Ouray SAR below me and then reached the top of the snow ramp below the first pitch of The Ribbon. Ouray SAR put me on a tether as I crawled on hands and knees to a waiting litter. SAR smoothly lowered me down to the creek and then raised me up the other side of the gulch. They transferred me to an ambulance, and eventually I reached a hospital in Montrose. I can never express enough gratitude for the men and women who showed up in that time of need. It's really important to give thanks to my partner. He was truly there when it mattered.

On the right leg, I broke my calcaneus, sprained the ankle, and damaged the nerve below the knee. On my left leg, I ruptured ligaments, had a significant ankle joint effusion, and partially tore the hamstring. I also partially tore my right bicep and have a left shoulder labrum tear. I'm healing well, all things considered.

ANALYSIS

During the second rappel, I was stepping over a bulge and I remember twisting my body to the right to see over my shoulder and find my feet in the dark. As I did this, the Munter hitch crept leftward toward the carabiner gate (*see figure A on facing page*). The rope rolled over the gate (unscrewing it in the process), popped it open, and undid itself from the carabiner. During my convalescence, I've been able to replicate this failure.

A different improvised rappel could have been used, but they all come with their own risks. If I use a Munter to rappel again, I'll use a twin-gate locking carabiner or an autolocking carabiner. I've already switched some important carabiners to twin gates or autolockers. *(Source: Nathan Chaszeyka.)*

**Editor's Note:* See Figure B on the facing page for an effective Munter hitch rappel. For details, Google "no twist munter hitch."

FALL ON ICE | Ice Screws Pulled Out

Vail, Rigid Designator Amphitheater

On December 14, I was stoked to get on Vail's newest pillar climb, Satan's Spear (WI5), after watching a couple of good friends send it. While climbing, I noticed how wet and slushy the ice had become near the top. My tools swung through the ice until the shafts were half buried and my feet kicked straight through. I downclimbed to my last screw and tried to back it up with another, but the ice there was also garbage; I could pull my screws straight out after they were over halfway in. I debated backing off and going down.

Around the corner farther left, I saw what looked like colder, more solid ice and decided to go for it. As I

The Spear (a.k.a. Satan's Spear)—the left of the two pillars—is a new, farmed ice route in the popular Rigid Designator Amphitheater. This climb was the site of a serious leader fall in December 2024. *Phil Wortmann*

made my way there, I again found myself fighting to find secure feet. They kept kicking through and cut out multiple times. I struggled to hang on to my tools. My feet cut one last time and I could no longer hang on. I fell, expecting to go about 20 feet into space.

Over the next couple of seconds, I saw the whole climb pass in front of my eyes. Two screws ripped out. Somewhere on the way down, I slammed into the pillar and smashed my arm. I fell about 80 feet before my belayer, Blake Hodges, caught me just off the deck. I felt like my arm had fallen off.

Not knowing the extent of my injuries, Blake immediately called paramedics. Every climber in the area seemed to have some level of medical training and came over to help. It was humbling to see everyone give up their day. Mountain rescue, paramedics, and a bunch of firefighters came up to help with evacuation. I spent a couple of nights in the hospital and had surgery on my left leg the next day.

ANALYSIS

I kept on climbing past what I knew was poor protection, "knowing" that I wouldn't fall. I even downclimbed to my last screw and debated bailing. I went against my first best judgment, thinking I could push through. *(Source: Pat Perry Johnson.)*

**Editor's Note:* Ice climbing is far less forgiving than rock. While protection can be very good, the medium is variable, and in poor ice protection cannot be relied on to catch a fall. A go-for-it attitude is rewarded on most forms of free climbing on rock. As we see here, going for it on ice often has higher consequences.

FREE SOLO FALLS

Boulder, Flatirons

On December 16, the Boulder County Sheriff's Office received a report that 42-year-old Keith Hayes had not returned home that evening after going climbing. Around 9 p.m., friends of Hayes' found his body near the top of the Second Flatiron, after presumably falling while unroped from Freezeway (5.7). His friends reported no sign of snow or ice on the route and that there was no sign of broken rock contributing to the fall.

The next day, December 17, a 27-year-old male was reported missing after not returning home in the evening from a Flatirons climb. The Boulder Emergency Squad found the body of the missing male a day later, after also presumably falling unroped, on the Standard East Face route (5.4) on the Third Flatiron. Rocky Mountain Rescue Group recovered the body after an eight-plus-hour operation.

ANALYSIS

Freezeway is a steep alternate finish to the Second Flatiron after completing one of several easier, low-angle east face routes. Hayes was very experienced and had climbed this route without a rope many times prior to his fall. The Standard East Face of the Third Flatiron, meanwhile, is one of the most popular beginner climbs in the U.S. and is frequently climbed unroped (though many climbers bring along a rope for the rappels from the top).

The accidents were a shock to the local community. The timing of both fatalities gained national attention. These tragedies serve as a reminder of the inherent risks of free solo climbing. Experience and fitness do not guarantee survival, and familiarity can degrade attentiveness. *(Sources: Friends of Keith Hayes and Bill Kinter.)*

CONNECTICUT

FALL ONTO LEDGE

Eastern Highlands, Ross Rocks

On November 24, Mason Amitrano (male, 28) was climbing Seeking Forgiveness (5.10) at the Gully Wall section of Ross Rocks, near the border between Connecticut and Rhode Island. Ross Rocks has a mix of sport and some trad routes. Seeking Forgiveness climbs past four bolts to reach a two-bolt anchor on a ledge at about 35 feet. Above the ledge, one can opt for a crack requiring trad gear, which climbs directly above the anchor and is now part of a route called Trad Direct, or opt for a traverse right to another sport route.

This very foreshortened view of the Gully Wall at Ross Rocks shows Seeking Forgiveness (5.10), marked in yellow. A crack finish above the two-bolt belay (blue X's) has no fixed gear, while the lower part has four bolts (blue X's). This discrepancy may have led a climber to continue up with no protection. ***Mike Ricard***

Amitrano fell from above the fourth bolt, hit the ledge, and continued falling for a total of 30 feet. It is unknown if he had clipped the two-bolt anchor on his way above the ledge. He had serious injuries to his skull, neck, elbow, and internal abdomen. First responders of the Danielson Technical Rescue Team, local fire departments, and police responded. Amitrano was stabilized and lowered in a litter to a small boat on Furnace Pond. He was transferred to UMass Memorial Hospital via a LifeFlight helicopter. Amitrano received intensive medical care for 60 days and is undergoing the long road to recovery.

ANALYSIS

On ClimbRI.org, Seeking Forgiveness is described as a former trad climb to which the anchor was added to make it fully sport. The description states that there are "bolts up to the anchor on the ledge where the sport climb ends. Or you can choose to continue up the crack (trad gear 5.10) to the shared anchor on Trad Direct [to the left]." It's reasonable to speculate that Amitrano expected to find more bolts—and it's not unreasonable for Amitrano to have expected them.

Areas with mixed sport and trad routes require extra attention. Researching objectives is imperative to discern where and on what routes trad gear is necessary. *(Sources: Dan Majercik, Quiet Corner Alerts, ClimbRI.org, and the Editors.)*

MASSACHUSETTS

SHORT FALL TO GROUND | Rope Severed by Rock Edge

Farley Ledges, Pot Ledge Buttress

On May 11, Tom Neary and his brother Paul were checking out a new boulder. At the top, they tied their 9.5mm dynamic rope to a tree. This created two lengths of rope with both ends reaching the ground. This allowed them to simultaneously rappel and clean moss and dirt from the 20-foot-plus boulder. The first 10 to 12 feet of the rock were overhanging. At the lip, the angle dramatically kicked back to a slab. This juncture of overhang and slab formed a straight, horizontal edge whose exterior angle was around 60°.

As two climbers were cleaning a boulder, one fell to the ground after his fixed rope was severed by the sawing motion of the weighted rope running across the coarse and acutely angled edge. *Tom Neary*

While on rappel and cleaning below the lip, Paul slid sideways. The brand-new rope, tensioned under body weight, was pulled across the edge. It cleanly and completely severed. The younger Neary fell four feet, landing on flat rocks below the boulder. He thankfully suffered only minor injuries.

ANALYSIS

It's never a good idea to run a rope, especially a dynamic rope, over an acute edge. While these climbers felt the lip was not extremely sharp, they did not account for the sliding motion of the rope going back and forth. On occasion, a climber might fall or lower over a sharp edge, but the force is not often concentrated on the isolated radius while loaded. In this case, the side-to-side motion acted like a saw blade.

Here we can see the fuzz left by the rope sheath. *Tom Neary*

There have been several fatalities over the years when a tensioned rope—often with a climber jumaring on one end—severed over an edge. By way of experiment, one can saw a tensioned rope across the edge of a brick (a mere 90° angle). The rope will cut in less than a minute. When ascending or working on a fixed line, a static rope is much less susceptible to abrasion or cutting over edges. *(Sources: Tom Neary and the Editors.)*

FATAL FALL ON RAPPEL | Lost Control of Rope

Leominster State Forest, Crow Hill

On July 11, RC (male, 69) and Joel were climbing at Crow Hill, a popular area with 100-foot-high cliffs. Both climbers were familiar with the area and quite experienced. They climbed pitch one of Outersite (5.7), then followed a bushy, left-trending ramp and finishing on pitch two of The Chimney (5.6). RC led the route in a single pitch. As Joel followed, he was stung several times by wasps. To avoid more stings, RC lowered Joel to the ground from mid-height. RC elected to rappel and retrieve two cams remaining in the final slot of The Chimney.

Rappelling this link-up was complicated. There is no fixed anchor on top of The Chimney. That route's exit slot and the left-trending ramp below prevented a straight-down rappel. RC chose to build a rappel anchor 20 feet to climber's right of the top of The Chimney. He girth-hitched a tree with his PAS and two locking carabiners. RC was known to be safe and conscientious.

Starting the rappel, RC lost control, falling 120 feet to the base and tumbling before coming to rest on the trail. Joel initiated CPR but discontinued due to RC's extensive trauma. The police eventually arrived at the scene of the fatal incident.

ANALYSIS

RC's rope had been pulled down from the anchor, with a large amount of slack tangled in the trees. The rope was partly draped on the cliff above, and the rappel anchor was intact. The carabiners at the anchor were still locked.

RC's partner reports that the fallen climber had failed to thread both rope strands through his rappel device. As the single strand was weighted, the other end slid through the anchor. He had recently begun using a "third hand" prusik as a backup, but it was a new technique and not yet second nature. He may have been distracted by the heat, the cam retrieval, and certainly concerned by the angry wasps.

Safe rappelling is dependent on a sound anchor and execution (*see page 12*). When you set up the rappel, make sure both strands are through the rappel device. Use stopper knots in both ends of the rope and be sure both ends reach the ground or the next anchor. Use a prusik or other third hand to back up your manual control of the rope. Double check your setup and, when possible, have a partner also check it. *(Sources: Joel and Christopher McKenzie, Massachusetts State Police, and the Editors.)*

MONTANA

FATAL FALL | Unroped

Glacier National Park, Livingston Range, Heavens Peak

On August 18, Grant Marcuccio (32) and a partner summited Heavens Peak (8,987 feet) at around 11:30 a.m. On that day, Marcuccio's plan was to summit the adjacent McPartland Mountain (8,417 feet) and then return to rejoin his partner. After that, they planned to descend to the highway.

Marcuccio departed Heavens Peak around 12:35 p.m., heading south to the adjacent summit. Sometime after, he elected to remove his backpack, possibly to lighten his load during the traverse. He was not using technical gear or a rope. Either on his way to or coming back from the summit of McPartland, Marcuccio slipped and fell to his death. His partner waited until about 8 p.m. When it became apparent that Marcuccio wouldn't return before dark, the waiting climber descended, got to cell service, and called SAR. After a weeklong search, the missing climber's body was found.

McPartland Mountain (8,417 feet) is one of many striking summits in Glacier National Park. In August 2024, the highly consequential terrain pictured here claimed the life of a very experienced climber who had previously summited 128 peaks in the area. *Anonymous*

ANALYSIS

Marcuccio was adept in this terrain and good at route-finding and reading the rock. He had previously climbed McPartland and his friends noted that the terrain between that summit and Heavens Peak involved 5th-class downclimbing. His friends strongly speculate that this accident was not the result of a route-finding error, but rather an unfortunate instance of slipping or tripping.

This and similar incidents in this book (*see page 56*) result in part from momentary inattention combined with loose rock and slick gravel. Locals note that very little climbing in Glacier National Park is done with protection due to the abysmal rock quality. One wrote to *ANAC*: "We go to great lengths to find [navigable] routes through and around these peaks. They are often exposed scrambles."

Surviving friends add:

- Though it would not have altered the outcome, having an inReach with live tracking would have saved Marcuccio's family and friends the week-long agony of not knowing where he had come to rest. It also would have reduced the resources needed to locate him.
- It is easy to say, "Don't solo!"—but there's no certainty that being with a partner would have changed the outcome.
- It is possible that the body recovery would have been much quicker had Marcuccio worn bright-colored clothing as it would have been easier to spot from a helicopter. *(Source: Anonymous.)*

KNEE STUCK IN CRACK

Gallatin Canyon, Sparerib Area

On August 15, two teams of two climbers were on the second pitch of a classic two-pitch crack called Sparerib (5.8). Climber 1 of the higher team led the pitch and brought up their partner, Climber 2. While following, Climber 2 got her knee stuck in the crux wide crack about five meters below the top. Meanwhile, Climbers 3 and 4 had arrived at the top of the first pitch.

Climbers 3 and 4 rappelled to the base, and Climber 4 ran down to the car to grab dish soap while Climber 3 hiked up the descent route to the top of the formation. Climber 3 helped Climber 1 put the belay ATC in guide mode, clipped directly to the anchor. Climber 3 then rappelled to the stuck climber to provide her with water, ibuprofen, and snacks. They cut the pants from the stuck knee using scissors from their first-aid kit.

In August, a climber got a knee stuck high on a two-pitch route in Gallatin Canyon. Here, she gets help from a fellow climber. She was freed in a few hours and finished the route. *Climber 1*

The time was 1:30 p.m., and the group was unsure if they could free Climber 2 before sunset. They activated an inReach satellite communicator, sent an SOS message, and got in touch with local SAR. They conveyed the appropriate information via text and were notified that a SAR team was on the way. Climber 4, having retrieved dish soap from the car, walked to the top and rappelled in. After slippery dish soap was rubbed around the knee, Climber 2 was able to extricate herself. Her total time stuck in the offwidth was about three hours.

The group messaged SAR that assistance was no longer needed. They then ascended to the top of the climb. Climber 1 recalled, "After her knee released, we offered to haul or help her jug a fixed rope, but she preferred to finish the route on her own power." There was minor bruising around Climber 2's knee, but no major injury.

ANALYSIS

Incidents involving stuck knees are not uncommon. This team did everything right. Their successful self-rescue resulted from collective experience, fortitude, and a little pluck. The group was well prepared to help the stuck climber, and fortunately they had dish soap in their vehicle. The Garmin inReach and scissors from the first-aid kit were valuable to have on hand. *(Source: Climber 1.)*

Red Rock Canyon lies just outside the Las Vegas metropolitan area. This proximity belies the remote wilderness setting in which rescues are often complex and hazardous. *BLM Nevada*

NEVADA

LEADER FALL ON ROCK | Protection Pulled Out

Red Rock Canyon National Conservation Area, Oak Creek Canyon

On November 10, I, Eric Chaudhary, and a partner (male, 26) were climbing Marijuana (5 pitches, 11c) in the Black Orpheus Amphitheater. My partner was leading the second pitch (10b). It exits hard left off a hanging belay with one bolt for protection about six feet above and ten feet to the left of the belay. The route then cuts back right to a roof/bulge, where I believe he placed a Black Diamond number 0.3 Z4 cam.

He did the move, manteled up, and was getting his stance when his foot slipped and he fell. The piece in the roof ripped, causing him to fall about six feet before being caught by the rope clipped to the first bolt. His ankle snagged and flipped him aggressively. The first thing that struck the wall was his head. He was wearing a helmet.

He was unconscious and hanging upside down approximately ten feet to my left and four feet above me. I lowered him to a small ledge that flipped him upright. He was now level with me. I then tied off the rope with a Munter-mule hitch and took him off belay. I called 911 (spotty reception) and relayed our location. I then yelled to a party of hikers or climbers at the base of the canyon. I informed them we needed helicopter rescue and that I was not sure if EMS had received my location.

I then basically lassoed my partner with a coil of rope and pulled him to me at the belay. Around then he started regaining consciousness. I secured him to the anchor, untied him, and set up a rappel. We then did a tandem rappel to the base of the first pitch with him attached to me. Luckily, we had twin 60-meter ropes.

At the actual base of the climb there is one belay bolt, but unfortunately it was too high to utilize as an anchor for the low-5th-class slab below. I built a two-piece gear anchor to descend that 150-foot lower section that comprises the approach to the first pitch. As we were rappelling, a SAR member yelled from the base of the canyon. I told him my partner was in and out of consciousness and we needed helicopter rescue. I finished the rap to a large ledge system. Five minutes later, a helicopter arrived. They flew out my partner and then returned for the SAR team member and me. My injured partner was diagnosed with a brain injury and ended up spending two weeks in the ICU.

ANALYSIS

I inspected the cam that blew, and it had a gouge in two of the lobes. The next party to climb the route retrieved our bail anchor. I was told that the spot where the piece had blown had no fresh scar. I'm still not sure why it didn't hold and hope to climb the route again to inspect it. *(Source: Eric Chaudhary.)*

**Editor's Note:* Fortunately, Chaudhary was very competent and effected an efficient self-rescue. Had he not descended to a helicopter-accessible area, the rescue might have taken many hours longer, and on a day when sunset was 4:30 p.m. Although close to Las Vegas, many parts of Red Rock are remote and have little or no cell phone service. Climbers should consider carrying an emergency satellite communication device.

NEW HAMPSHIRE

LONG LEADER FALL ON ICE

Crawford Notch State Park, Mt. Webster

On December 14, Slavek Zaglewski (55) was climbing Shoestring Gully (WI2 M2) with his friend Mariusz Markewicz. This long, moderate climb starts as a snow gully and steepens through several ice steps before finishing via a classic mixed exit.

In the late afternoon, Zaglewski fell 60 feet while leading a chimney near the top. Despite wearing a helmet, he suffered severe head injuries and was unconscious and unable to move. Markewicz anchored Zaglewski in a secure position.

Having no cell service, Markewicz soloed the final section in darkness to reach the rim on Mt. Webster. Around 7 p.m., he was able to call 911. With temperatures falling into the teens, a New Hampshire Fish and Game SAR team responded along with two dozen volunteers from the Mountain Rescue Service (MRS) and Androscoggin Valley SAR (AVSAR).

MRS team members climbed the gully to reach Zaglewski at 11:19 p.m. They began treatment for hypothermia. On December 15 at 12:46 a.m., AVSAR descended with a litter and raised him 400 feet to the rim. Zaglewski was

New Hampshire's Mt. Webster offers moderate multipitch ice routes with a distinctly alpine feel. In December 2024 a climber fell while leading a mixed chimney (seen here in fat conditions) on a route called Shoestring Gully. The ensuing overnight rescue took place in very cold conditions. *Robert Hall*

carried two miles down the steep trail, arriving at a waiting ambulance at 5 a.m.

The following day he was transferred from a North Conway hospital to an ICU in Portland, Maine. His injuries included fractured neck vertebrae, rib and nose fractures, a severe concussion, lacerations, and cold-weather injuries. He remembered nothing of his accident until three weeks later. Six months later, he was still dealing with frostbitten fingers that would require partial amputation.

ANALYSIS

Zaglewski had climbed Shoestring Gully twice before, and it was well within his ability. At the time of the accident, there was less ice than usual due to a warm autumn. The difficult conditions contributed to his fall.

Falls on alpine terrain are always serious. Place protection where you can. Early-season ice and mixed climbs often require rock protection, ice hooks, and possibly pitons for iced-in cracks.

Hypothermia is a secondary risk in winter climbing, and this hazard increases when one is rendered inactive due to trauma. A climber's relative physical fitness has little influence on the onset speed of hypothermia. Despite the fast response and sizable rescue resources, Zaglewski was immobile for six hours. He also believes he may have removed his gloves due to the paradoxic hot sensation sometimes felt by victims of extreme hypothermia.

This remarkable overnight rescue prevented a worse outcome. Zaglewski said in a newspaper article, "My rescuers are amazing. I owe my life to them." *(Sources: Slavek Zaglewski, Sgt. Alex Lopashanski, New Hampshire Fish and Game, and Clara Cousins.)*

NEW MEXICO

FALL ON ROCK

Sandias, Muralla Grande

On August 6, Eben (42) and Stewart (32) hiked down the Chimney Canyon Trail at 8:49 a.m. to get to the base of The Second Coming (4 pitches, 5.8) on Muralla Grande. Eben had nine years of climbing experience and was training and mentoring Stewart in trad climbing. They'd climbed easy to moderate routes in the Sandias and both felt prepared for the route, having swapped leads of that grade during the year.

Eben started leading the first pitch at 9:30 a.m. Stewart led the second, finishing on a two-foot-wide ledge. They took a short break. Eben had climbed the route with a guide in 2016 and remembered the third pitch as being difficult and heady. The crux comes at a right-traversing ledge where the leader has to commit to a slightly overhanging hand crack in a left-facing dihedral.

Eben attempted the traverse at 11:30 a.m. It was hot and the dihedral was in the full sun. The hand crack proved challenging, with bad/insecure feet. Eben placed a marginal number 3 Dragon Cam at the crux and went left for a chalked two-finger pocket. After a few attempts his feet slipped and he fell 15 feet. All gear held, but Eben's left foot had caught a small ledge while he was falling and there was extreme pain in his left ankle. It was around 12:30 p.m. and the pair determined he likely had broken bones. Self-rescue was discussed but there were no rappel anchors in the area, so it would have meant committing to four or five rappels over difficult terrain. A rappel retreat would also have meant hiking out on the steep Chimney Canyon Trail.

With good cell coverage, they called 911. At some point a SAR drone flew above. The SAR team constructed a rope system at the top of the cliff, and 4.5 hours later, Albuquerque Mountain Rescue lowered in.

Ultimately, Stewart and one SAR member were lowered to the base while the injured Eben and a second SAR member were hauled out. They arrived at the top of the cliff at 7 p.m. At an Albuquerque hospital, Eben was diagnosed with a broken left fibula and talus.

ANALYSIS

Climbing in the Sandias is an adventure and the climbing grades are considered "stout." Some would consider the dihedral where Eben fell as 5.9, which was his trad leading limit. Tape or hand jammies would have provided a sense of security for his sweaty hands in the direct sun. It was fortunate they had a cell signal and enough daylight to summon SAR and be successfully rescued. *(Source: Eben Travis.)*

NEW YORK

STRANDED | No Equipment, Off Route

Adirondacks, Mt. Colden

On October 12, dispatch received a call from two climbers on the Trap Dike. The pair was unable to move due to steep rock and wet conditions. New York State Police Aviation was called to fly three forest rangers to the location to perform a technical rope rescue. It was too wet and unsafe to rescue the pair from below, so rangers climbed to the top of the dike and rappelled down to the subjects.

At 5:30 p.m., rescuers reached the two scramblers who were from Québec. After the climbers were secured, they were lowered. Rangers warmed and fed them, took the pair across the lake by boat, and hiked with them to Marcy Dam. The subjects reached their vehicles at the trailhead at 2:45 a.m.

The Trap Dike starts in a dike gully (pictured here) before exiting onto a slab leading to the summit of Mt. Colden. This popular route, part scramble and part technical climb, has been the scene of many rescues over the years. *New York State Department of Environmental Conservation*

ANALYSIS

The Trap Dike is a 2,000-foot-long moderate climb with a 30-foot technical rock step near a waterfall. In winter the route becomes a technical ice and snow climb. It is the scene of recurring rescues when scramblers exit the 4th-class dike too early and end up stranded on 5th-class slabs. Typically, the people who are stranded do not self-identify as climbers. However, in this case the two subjects (male, 42, and female, 43) were climbers but had not intended to do a technical route and thus had no equipment. *(Source: New York State Department of Environmental Conservation.)*

SHAWANGUNKS ANNUAL SUMMARY

The 2024 season at the Mohonk Preserve saw numerous climbing-related incidents that resulted in various musculoskeletal injuries. There were eight lead climbing incidents, four bouldering accidents, and one environmental incident that the Mohonk SAR rangers responded to. (The environmental incident was a climber who sustained a copperhead snakebite.) Throughout the course of 2024, the Mohonk Preserve rangers conducted several preventive search and rescue (PSAR) clinics to help people understand and prepare for the various conditions they might encounter. *(Source: Mohonk Preserve Rangers.)*

ROCKFALL | Rock Dislodged During Intentional Fall

Shawangunks, Trapps Area

On October 2, a male climber was practicing lead climbing falls on the second pitch of Frog's Head (5.6). To protect these falls, the climber used a fixed piece alongside several pieces placed in and around a protruding feature. From above the gear, the climber deliberately took multiple leader falls. He had been practicing this skill following a "Fall Therapy" clinic that was taught indoors by a certified guide.

In October, a climber was taking practice falls after attending a "Fall Therapy" clinic that was taught indoors by a certified guide. This led to a serious accident when a chunk of rock was dislodged, striking the climber after he stopped falling. The above rock weighs about 1,000 pounds and represents half of the falling rock, which broke upon impact with the ground. *Mohonk Preserve*

After at least one fall, the climber ascended and fell again, intending to be caught by the same cluster of gear. However, the force of falling dislodged a large piece of the rock feature where the gear had been placed. As he fell, the rock struck the climber in the face and head. The climber's fall was eventually arrested by his next closest piece of gear.

Despite wearing a helmet, the climber was rendered unconscious and suspended upside down by the rope. The climber's belayer held the fall but was otherwise unable to take further action to assist the climber.

Mohonk SAR rangers were promptly

The Mohonk Preserve in the Shawangunks protects one of America's premier climbing areas. Rangers respond to numerous climbing accidents every year. *Grendelkhan—Wikimedia*

notified and responded. Due to the location of the patient, the SAR team accessed the site from the top of the cliff. Upon reaching the climber, the SAR ranger identified that the patient was not breathing adequately and quickly repositioned him to open the airway. The patient was also bleeding significantly from the wounds on his head caused by the falling rock. The ranger performed a "pickoff" maneuver to free the climber from the rope and bring him to the ground. Further personnel with a rescue litter performed a hasty carry-out operation. The patient was then transported to an ambulance and was subsequently transferred to a medevac.

ANALYSIS

While it is common for climbers to take leader falls on traditional gear in the Gunks, intentional lead falls are less typical. This incident highlights the potential risks of applying indoor training techniques to outdoor environments. Outdoor climbing demands full consideration of many aspects not found indoors. In this case, specific gear placements, interpretation of terrain features, and choosing what to fall on all came into play. This accident underscores the importance of carefully inspecting the rock and surrounding features before committing to falls.

Additionally, the potential absence of a pre-established "worst-case scenario" plan and clear communication between the climber and belayer may have contributed to the severity of the incident. Climbers should have a mutual understanding of risk management and safety measures, especially in an outdoor environment. This might include how to anchor an unconscious climber in order to release the belayer. *(Source: Mohonk Preserve Rangers.)*

FALL ON ROCK | Lowering Error, Clipped Wrong Rope at Anchor

Shawangunks, The Near Trapps Area

On October 14, Mohonk SAR rangers responded to a climber who had fallen to the ground while being lowered from Outer Space (5.8) in the Near Trapps area. They found the climber (Climber 2, female) lying in the talus beneath the route. A trailing rope was threaded through the lead protection and the route's anchor above.

Outer Space is a single-pitch climb that has an unusually long, left-trending traverse that ends at the anchor. Climber 2 was part of a three-person team. One party member led the route, clipped the anchor, and was lowered to the ground. As follower, Climber 2 was tied in to the middle of the rope. They followed the pitch while being belayed from the ground on the leader's side of the rope. As they followed, Climber 2 left the lead protection in place, unclipping their overhead rope and then clipping the trailing side of the rope into the protection. This procedure was intended to protect the third climber (Climber 3), who would subsequently follow the pitch. Re-clipping ensured that Climber 3 would not take a long pendulum fall if they came off.

Climber 2 reached the top. They unlocked the anchor carabiners and unclipped their side of the rope. They then clipped the trailing (unbelayed) side of the rope into the anchor. In doing so, Climber 2 essentially took themselves off belay. When they leaned back to lower, they fell over 60 feet directly to the ground. They landed between several rocks at the base.

Rangers assessed Climber 2, and besides finding some minor lacerations, they identified a significant spinal injury in the upper lumbar region. A carry-out was executed, and the climber was littered out to the trail entrance and transported to the hospital.

ANALYSIS

Climber 2 failed to recognize that unclipping the belayed side of the rope left them completely unbelayed. Two factors—slingshot top-roping in a party of three and the unusually long traverse—led to this uncommon rope configuration. Climber 2 essentially mimicked the actions of a lead climber while pulling up slack and re-clipping the trailing rope. This might have led to a lead climbing mindset and a subconscious impression that they were to be lowered after re-clipping the anchor.

Unclipping and re-clipping protection to safeguard a third climber is a technique more often used on multipitch climbs. It appears that the two followers did not fully understand the system, nor its nuances. Clear, precise communication among all team members is essential for safety, especially when using complex and unfamiliar systems. The belayer (who had led the pitch) reported that Climber 2 struggled to unclip the two opposite and opposed lockers at the anchor. This struggle should have been a warning. Whether based on their own observation or by the instruction of the group leader, the third climber could have put a belay on the trailing end of rope.

Understanding systems and associated risks can prevent accidents. In this case, Climber 3 deferred to the experience of the group leader. Climbers should be encouraged to speak up and ask questions (*see: The Partner Dynamic, page 23*). The group leader should ensure that all present comprehend the plan before starting. *(Source: Mohonk Preserve Rangers.)*

NORTH CAROLINA

LEDGE FALL

Pisgah National Forest, Looking Glass Rock, Fate Osteen Crag

AH (37) and CE (48) met online and decided to go to the Fate Osteen Crag for some rock climbing. On November 29, they got to the base of Twist of Fate (2 pitches, 5.7) and decided that CE would lead the first pitch (5.7). AH joined CE at the belay. To get more experience, AH also decided to lead the first pitch. Both climbers descended, and AH led it with no issues. CE followed and checked her gear placements.

AH wanted to lead the second pitch, also 5.7, but had some trepidation. With positive encouragement from CE, she started up, placing gear and moving well. When she got to the headwall crux, she placed Black Diamond 0.2 and 0.4 cams. As she began the sequence, she became nervous and downclimbed a short distance. She then fell about 20 feet, impacting the ledge below.

AH sustained an open fracture of one leg and asked to be lowered. At the belay, CE used his shirt to help manage the bleeding. CE texted the Transylvania County Rescue Squad via iPhone SOS and lowered AH to the ground. CE then rappelled.

On the ground, they did rudimentary first aid on the open ankle fracture. They attempted to hike out but quickly realized it would be too difficult and that it would do more damage to the ankle. AH waited as CE went to meet the rescuers. AH was carried out on a Sked and later a Stokes basket. She refused pain meds and went into surgery the next morning.

ANALYSIS

North Carolina has areas where slabs angle up before meeting steeper sections of rock. Slack often builds up and rope drag is generated, as the climber moves up—usually into a crux. All that, combined with the slab below, adds up to a bad ledge fall.

Moving the belay to the base of the headwall would have reduced rope stretch and allowed for a closer belay. Most climbers do not consider belaying outside the "normal" (guidebook) locations, especially if those established belays are bolted.

One can also place more and/or higher gear when climbing above a slab. AH did well to place two pieces before the crux. She also combined them with an "alpine equalization," sharing the load between the two pieces by clipping one directly to the other. One of her cams was solid while the other was under-cammed. Thinking ahead may well have prevented a longer fall. *(Sources: Karsten Delap and the Editors.)*

FALL ON ROCK | Protection Pulled Out

Linville Gorge, Table Rock Mountain

On August 2, I took a 20-foot whipper on Her Route (5.9) after my last piece blew. The route was at the upper end of my lead ability, and I knew very little about it. A group of Outward Bound students was top-roping nearby, and I was reaching my physical limit when one of the students fell and screamed. The sound led me to fall.

I am low-assistance-required autistic and more sound-sensitive than most people. The scream startled me, and the need for emotional regulation made falling or hanging inevitable (*see "Climbing and Autism" below*). I gave my belayer notice

On August 2, a climber fell while leading a route on Table Rock Mountain. She was unaware of it at the time, but she had broken her back. Despite the injury, she self-rescued shortly before a thunderstorm doused the crag (seen above). *Anonymous Climber*

and placed a poor microcam, hoping it would hold body weight. I slipped and fell, rotating to the right. The cam didn't hold, but the nut placed beneath it did. I hit the rock hard, striking my head and the right side of my upper back. In the process, I destroyed my helmet. One witness said I lost consciousness.

Immediately after the fall, I knew something was injured. It also started raining. Without hesitation, I downclimbed until I could get to the bolt anchor on an adjacent route. I then brought my partner up. We simul-rappelled 60 feet to a ledge from where we could scramble to the ground. We walked back to the parking lot in the pouring rain. I made it to the hospital, where I was diagnosed with compression fractures from T8 through T10.

ANALYSIS

The climb went well until I moved a bit off route to the left. When I heard the scream, I was struggling to find a way up. A good cam placement was not possible because of lichen and the flare of the crack. I've fallen multiple times leading and suffered nothing more than a scrape or bruise. This time I knew I was seriously injured. It might have been a fatal fall had I not been wearing a helmet. I've always told my partners that I won't get on a climb that I can't get both of us off of. But I never expected to do it in these conditions. *(Source: Climber.)*

**Editor's Note*: Credit goes to this climber for her knowledge of the area and ability to self-rescue, especially considering her extensive injuries. It's good to know how to rescue your partner and yourself. Building an anchor, escaping a belay (load transfer), rappelling, and ascending fixed ropes are essential elements.

CLIMBING AND AUTISM

In an article at UKClimbing.com, a climber with autism describes how the sport has helped them lean into their difference. Search "Unmasked—Climbing and Autism" to find it. In autism spectrum disorder, *low-assistance-required* refers to autistic individuals with a relatively mild presentation of autistic traits and who require minimal external support to function independently. *Regulation* refers to the ability to manage and respond to emotions, behaviors, and in this case, sensory experiences.

The rugged Linville Gorge is a quality Southeastern climbing destination and also a designated wilderness area. The relative isolation of these crags needs consideration when planning a climb. ***Ken Thomas—Wikimedia***

LONG PENDULUM FALL

Linville Gorge, Amphitheater

On January 19, MC and FC started their approach to the Amphitheater to climb The Daddy (500 feet, 5.6). They parked at the seasonally locked gate below the Table Rock Recreation Area and hiked to the Amphitheater, adding three miles (an extra hour or two) to the round trip. The weather was good when they left the car. However, upon their arrival at the base of the climb later in the day, the wind was increasing and the temperature was dropping.

The pair climbed the first pitches without incident. While following the penultimate pitch, FC fell, swinging across the face. She tumbled, rolled, and struck her left leg on sharp rock. She stopped below MC, with a laceration below her left knee and bruises to her right leg. MC lowered her to a ledge. She attended to her wound as MC rebuilt the anchor and rappelled to her. They fashioned a compression dressing using a sling and a hat and called 911. Then MC ascended the rappel rope and created a mechanical advantage system to assist FC up to his stance with overhead tension. He then led the remainder of the route and used the same system to assist FC to the top. Upon completing the climb, they notified 911 that they were on top.

Rescuers en route knew the weather was getting worse. They advised the pair to walk to the main Amphitheater trail. The rescuers reached the climbers approximately an hour after dark. They were able to manage FC's injuries and provide both climbers with food, hydration, and more clothing layers. The group arrived at the trailhead at 7:45 p.m. The temperature had dropped to 18°F with wind of 20 mph and blowing snow. FC went to the ER and received 14 stitches.

ANALYSIS

Wind, ice, cold rock, low light, and other environmental factors may have contributed to FC's fall. January has short days, and the local forecast called for cold temperatures, high winds, and snow later in the day. This should have been enough to cancel the climb. Neither climber had enough gear or food to spend the night. Fortunately, MC had the knowledge and ability to successfully self-rescue the team to the top of the climb. *(Sources: Jon Massey, James Robinson, Burke County SAR, and the Editors.)*

FALL ON ROCK

Blue Ridge Mountains, Laurel Knob

On October 19, two climbers set off to climb Fathom, an eight-pitch 5.10a slab route on Laurel Knob. The lead climber had four years of multipitch experience. He planned to have his partner lead the initial pitch, but upon their arrival, the climb appeared manageable enough for an onsight.

Starting up, the lead climber placed solid protection in horizontal cracks and reached a rest 35 feet above the ground. Here the climbing became trickier. There were two apparent options: a direct line on friction over a bulge or a shallow, unprotected depression to the left. The belayer suggested placing a backup cam and taking the easier (left) option. The leader struggled to figure out the traverse. He then signaled to his partner that he was going to take the direct line.

After some tenuous moves, he climbed ten feet above his last placement. Then he lost traction and fell. The belayer took in slack and braced as the lead climber tumbled 20 feet, impacting his left ankle and stopping 15 to 20 feet off the ground. Initially feeling unhurt, he soon noticed pain in his ankle. They decided to abandon the climb.

ANALYSIS

Assessment: Although the first pitch appeared straightforward, the challenging terrain wasn't apparent until mid-pitch. The leader could have downclimbed to his protection to traverse or retreat.

Communication and Preferences: The belayer was the more experienced climber and was cautious about giving beta or making suggestions. The leader was accustomed to getting more guidance. He would have benefitted from understanding their different approaches to communication and giving beta.

Skill and Difficulty Match: Although excited by the manageable appearance of the first pitch, he might have been better served to have his partner lead. He emailed *ANAC*, "I think the low angle does make it look easier, but I've had to bail off other routes on Laurel Knob. I have a healthy respect for North Carolina slab." *(Source: Lead Climber.)*

BOULDERING FALL | Missed the Pads

Crowders Mountain State Park, Dixon School Boulders

On February 18, my friend and I (Anonymous) hiked to the Dixon School Boulders for a session. We'd been climbing there for a number of years. After warming up in the Lower Patio Area, we went to the classic Galvatron (V3). Since we often climb

Laurel Knob is one of the tallest crags in the eastern U.S. and home to some serious multipitch climbing. Formerly a clandestine climbing destination on private land, the 1,200-foot granite dome was purchased by the Carolina Climbers Coalition in 2006. Fathom (5.10a) takes the big right-trending dihedral. ***Tim Wheatley***

together, I know my partner tends to fall off to the side of this problem. I tend to fall straight down. Normally there's a third pad covering the seam between our two pads, but this time we didn't have it. We also didn't see the pine needles that had accumulated on the finish—they caused me to slip off the slopey top-out, and I fell about 12 feet. I was ready to roll and aim for my pad, but my heels landed in the seam, injuring my left foot.

I quickly elevated my feet, took off my climbing shoes, and got out my first-aid kit. After taking some pain meds, I wrapped my left foot. I had a pair of high-top hiking shoes and put those on tight. After some of the pain passed, I tried to stand, but that was a big NO!

My partner carried the pads back to the car while I crawled on my knees and scooted on my butt about a mile. I didn't have any displacement, so thankfully didn't need surgery. I was diagnosed with bilateral calcaneus fractures and had air casts on both feet for two months.

ANALYSIS

The two of us had completed this problem before, and the familiarity gave us a false sense of security. I had climbed on Galvatron alone with my usual three-pad set. On those occasions, I had my thick pad closer to the problem. On accident day, my partner's thinner pad was up close while mine was farther back than usual. The top has slopers, and the pine needles didn't help—it would have been good to inspect the top instead of just jumping on the problem. *(Source: Anonymous.)*

OREGON

NEAR MISS | Open Grigri

Climbing Gym

On March 24, while at a rock gym, Bystander 1 and Bystander 2 were alerted by a belayer that he needed assistance. A climber was top-roping near the end of a route and the belayer's Grigri was not fully closed. This left the outer plate open and the rope exposed.

This re-creation shows an unclosed Grigri during a simulated belay. Note that the rope can remain threaded while the device is unclosed. A cursory visual assessment may not reveal that the device is open. *Ruby Piechocki*

The belayer told the climber to stay in place and started to remove the rope from the Grigri while placing the lower portion of the rope under his foot. Bystander 1 grabbed the rope above the belayer's head to help safeguard the climber. Bystander 2 took a segment of the rope and threaded it into a separate Grigri to put the climber back on belay. Bystander 2 then pulled in the slack and safely lowered the climber to the floor. Both the belayer and the climber appeared to be experienced and familiar with the Grigri and both claimed that a safety check had been performed before the climber started up. No one was hurt.

ANALYSIS

Complacency or distraction led to the belayer's Grigri being unsecured. This could have led to the rope popping out of the device and potentially dropping the climber. Fortunately, Bystander 1 and Bystander 2 were close by, wearing harnesses, and had belay devices. The belayer's impulse to remove the rope from the Grigri might have resulted in a ground fall had Bystanders 1 and 2 not been able to intercede. Thorough safety checks with visual and verbalized confirmation would have prevented this near miss. Gym staff reviewed security camera footage and concluded that Bystander 1 and Bystander 2 took the proper action. *(Source: Ruby Piechocki.)*

FALL ON SNOW | Fumarole

Mt. Hood, South Side

On April 11, I (Ben Sleister) and my climbing partner were ascending the standard south-side route on Mt. Hood. There were at least three parties ahead of us. We had climbed/skied to the Devil's Kitchen area by around 7 a.m. The conditions were springlike after several days of warming and freeze-thaw. It was about 32°F, avalanche danger was low, and the weather clear. We both put on harnesses as a rescue precaution. I also carried a 30-meter rope for the same reason.

In April 2024, an 18-year-old climber tumbled into this fumarole after taking a long fall on Mt. Hood. He was discovered wedged between the rock and snow. His father/climbing partner can be seen descending (red circle) above. ***Ben Sleister***

We continued up at the same time as another party of two. Shortly after, I saw a climber falling down a steep section above, cartwheeling head over heels. The four of us had a brief discussion and I climbed up the slope toward the fallen climber. I arrived three to five minutes later.

The climber was standing on rock in the gap between a fumarole and the snowy rim. He had no apparent way out. I descended toward him, but when I got within 30 feet, the instability of the snow made me cautious. The climber was alert but could not get out of the pit. His face and jacket were covered with blood. He complained of finger and hand pain but no other injuries.

I attempted to place a picket but the snow was like ball bearings. My partner and I sat down and dug in with crampons to form an anchor. I lowered my rope to the climber with an ice axe attached. With the assistance of the rope, the stranded climber crawled and climbed out of the pit.

Another party above us had descended and they helped us get the injured climber to a safer location. (One of the rescuers departed after complaining of shortness of breath from the sulfur fumes emanating from the fumarole.) We assessed the climber and found no injuries besides a bleeding nose and finger pain. He was wearing a helmet, was 18 years old, and said that his dad was still at the top. We gave him some extra layers, water, and sugar and waited for his father. We discussed calling for a rescue but did not feel the injury warranted air evacuation. It took the climber's father 60 to 90 minutes to descend. By this time the fallen climber was feeling better and elected to descend with his father. We advised they visit a medical facility to assess for head trauma.

ANALYSIS

Deceptive conditions on the south side of Mt. Hood and a reputation as an "easy" route contributed to this accident. While Mt. Hood carries a stigma against roping up, the consequences of a fall can be fatal. The fallen climber was lucky to have survived—I estimate he had fallen over 1,000 feet. *(Source: Ben Sleister.)*

STRANDED | Locking Carabiner Jammed

Smith Rock State Park, Kiss of the Lepers Buttress

On December 22, at 4:51 p.m., I was dispatched to a stuck climber at Smith Rock State Park. A female climber was stuck about 40 feet above the ground on the final rappel from a route called First Kiss (5 pitches, 5.7). She was climbing with a male partner who was safely on the ground but unable to help. He had rappelled before her and she couldn't disconnect from the anchor.

The climber was anchored to a bolt with a PAS and she had no means of cutting the PAS. Mountain rescue was paged at 5:05 p.m. and 12 volunteers responded.

Our teams assisted the stranded climber by providing a pair of pliers to help release the stuck carabiner screwgate. She pulled it up to herself and was then able to continue safely to the ground and did not need further assistance.

ANALYSIS

It's silly that it took 12 SAR personnel to essentially unlock a stuck carabiner, but we wanted to be sure we had resources on hand in case the situation was worse than reported. *(Source: Caleb Bryce, Deschutes County Sheriff's Office Search and Rescue.)*

Editor's Note: This is a relatively rare case of equipment "failure," as the carabiner became fully locked shut, preventing the climber from removing her tether and continuing the rappel. The team leader inspected the carabiner and it was completely functional after being opened. Perhaps sand was caught in the screw mechanism. Sometimes, if the screw sleeve is tightened while the carabiner is under body weight, the sleeve can jam. Often, putting the carabiner under load and then turning the screw sleeve can release the gate.

An injured climber being evacuated from the base of Picnic Lunch Wall at Smith Rock. After this climber suffering a debilitating leader fall, he and his partner fixed their rope and rappelled two pitches to the base, thereby facilitating a faster and safer rescue. *Kassandra Spinnie*

LEADER FALL | Loose Rock

Smith Rock State Park, Picnic Lunch Wall

On June 13, Nolan (32) and I, Kassandra Spinnie (30), were climbing Voyage of the Cowdog (3 pitches, 5.9). It was well within our grade, as we had done numerous other multipitch routes at the same level and harder. We made it to the third pitch without difficulty. Nolan was about 60 feet up when a hold broke. He fell about 30 feet before the rope caught him. Due to his body position at the time of the hold breaking, Nolan fell sideways and slammed into the wall, his ankle and foot taking the brunt of the impact. I was able to lower him to the belay. We noted that he would be unable to walk out, and we decided SAR needed to be called.

Nolan activated his Garmin inReach, and we were able to communicate with dispatchers. I used a sweatshirt and some extra slings to create a splint. SAR determined it would be best if we could get to the base of the climb. Since we were two pitches up, the rope was not long enough for a typical rappel. I fixed the rope and rappelled the single rope, going first to ensure the rope would reach the base, and then Nolan rappelled. SAR was waiting to help him evacuate.

Nolan ended up with a displaced talar neck fracture in his foot that required emergent surgery. A kind party behind us was able to clean our gear and return it to us later that night.

ANALYSIS

Thinking back, we had all of our safeguards in place. Nolan had an inReach, which allowed for contact with SAR. An important thing is that rock climbing is dangerous, and no matter how well prepared or how confident you are, things can go wrong. It was good to have the necessary gear and skills to self-rescue. *(Sources: Kassandra Spinnie and Nolan's Instagram account.)*

STRANDED | Ropes Stuck

Smith Rock State Park, Smith Rock Group

On May 25 at 12:11 p.m., I (Caleb Bryce) was dispatched to two climbers who had gotten their ropes stuck while rappelling. The two subjects were not injured and were secure on a ledge. We reached the two subjects at 3:30 p.m., and both were safely on the ground less than two hours later.

The pair of young male climbers had completed a climb on the back side of the Smith Formation (Smith Rock Group). Rather than descend their ascent route, they tried to follow the rappel route for a popular climb called Wherever I May Roam. There are numerous bolts at the top of the formation, and they chose the incorrect route, rappelling off old bolts that were set back from an edge. This created a lot of friction and the pair were unable to pull their ropes.

Their station was under an overhang, and so we did not have visual or auditory contact from the top. We rigged for a pickoff. Because the subjects were off route, my rescue partner had to construct an intermediate anchor farther down the wall to act as an impromptu rappel station. I went back and cleaned this anchor a few weeks later.

A rescuer approaches two stranded climbers after they took the wrong descent and got their ropes stuck on a recessed anchor. Immediately prior, the pair had watched another party rappel off the same incorrect anchor, get their rope stuck (yellow oval), and abandon it. This rescued pair simply threaded their own rope on top of the abandoned rope, almost guaranteeing they would get stranded. *Deschutes County Sheriff's Office Search and Rescue*

ANALYSIS

It's very common to descend on the wrong route from this popular formation. The friction of the rappel rope on the edge, in addition to the wind, made rope retrieval impossible. The two climbers also lacked the gear and knowledge to ascend a double rope. They were completely dependent on our aid.

Always be certain of the correct rappel line before descending, or at the very least know how to ascend your ropes if necessary. Also, this team did not have adequate layers to be in the wind and shade. Even in a front-country destination like Smith, wind and exposure at a hanging belay can become quite serious. *(Source: Caleb Bryce, Deschutes County Sheriff's Office Search and Rescue.)*

SOUTH DAKOTA

AMPUTATION | Leader Fall, Rope Wrapped Around Pinkie

Spearfish Canyon, Warm-Up Walls

My partner and I, Spencer Drewelow (37), were climbing in Spearfish Canyon over the Labor Day weekend. On our third day of climbing, I tried to onsight Black Rainbow (11b), my third route of the day. The first half was on easier terrain, but on the second half the difficulty picked up.

I clipped the last bolt and paused to read the moves to the anchor. I made a move, but it didn't feel right so I reversed to an okay stance near the last bolt. Pausing, I looked for another sequence. The forearm pump was building, and I decided to go for it. The anchors were open-shuts, the kind where you drop the rope into the hooks. With my left hand on a crimp, I stepped up with my right foot on an edge. I bore down and as I was stepping up, I grabbed the rope with my right hand in order to clip above my head. I touched the rope to the shuts but was not able to drop it in. Then I fell.

Spencer Drewelow demonstrates how, while clipping an anchor in Spearfish Canyon, he fell and the rope amputated his pinkie. Reattachment surgery was successful, as was the follow-up leech therapy. His finger ultimately survived, and he is climbing again. *Spencer Drewelow*

As I fell, the slack looped and cinched around my right hand. My body weighted the rope and I bounced lightly off the wall, and then I knew something was wrong. At first I thought I had a really bad rope burn. Then I saw my right pinkie. It was dangling by a thin piece of skin. I gave out a loud roar, and my partner lowered me to the ground.

I sat down and fell into shock. A nearby climbing party heard us and came over. Fortunately, one of them was a doctor and bandaged my hand. It was a 20-minute hike down the trail and a half-hour drive to the hospital in Spearfish. The on-call orthopedic doctor performed basic surgery to reattach my finger. We considered a helicopter airlift, but ultimately they advised me it would be okay to drive home. My climbing partner drove us back to Colorado that night, and the next day, in Denver, I had an advanced emergency replant of the right pinkie.

ANALYSIS

It's not a good idea to fall with the rope in your hand. I had assessed that a fall would be clean, but when I made the move to the anchor, I felt a little desperate and did a little lunge. As I tried to clip the open-shut anchors, my right hand and wrist did a rotating motion, and performing this motion twisted the loop of rope around my hand.

A couple of things might have prevented this outcome, including finding a better clipping stance or climbing closer to the anchor to make the clip. Clipping above one's head adds a lot of slack to the system. This can create the opportunity for a limb to get caught and also will lengthen the fall. *(Source: Spencer Drewelow.)*

TEXAS

BOULDERING FALL | Poor Pad Placement

Hueco Tanks State Park, North Mountain

On January 22, I (Pete Korpics, 35) was attempting to climb a long-standing project called See Spot Run (V6). I was well aware of the risks involved and that it would require ample padding.

During previous sessions, I had placed six or more pads across a wide area, including the back of the fall zone. Six pads or more is ideal, but I was admittedly negligent on the day of the accident, as I felt I'd complete the route and was excited to do it. I also felt that the pad number and placement—five total and not as wide as on prior attempts—was adequate given the presence of two spotters.

I felt very strong getting to the crux. After pulling through the crux I got very pumped, lost momentum, and hesitated. We all know that moment when you feel uncertain about the next move. In

Pete Korpics on an early attempt on See Spot Run. He recalls, "I was very familiar with this famous and dangerous route, as I'd been attempting it for several years." ***Pete Takeda***

those moments we tell ourselves, "Do it anyway." Sometimes this works, but often it doesn't. In this case, I fell.

I fell from roughly 15 feet up, with quite a bit of force. My spotters were hesitant to put their bodies in harm's way. I had told them that above the crux, staying clear was the best thing to do. Having two people injured is worse than one.

Due to the momentum of the fall and the poor pad placement, my left foot hit the rock and my right foot hit the pad. I severely sprained my ankle. It was probably not helpful that it has in the past received the same injury.

ANALYSIS

Massively underreported in terms of accidents, bouldering is inherently dangerous, and highball problems particularly so. Besides being a four-star John Sherman classic, See Spot Run is a notorious ankle-breaker. At 25 feet tall it is described on MountainProject.com as "one of the more notorious highball problems at Hueco." During the same season Korpics had his accident, falls from the route caused multiple ankle sprains.

On highballs, the impact forces of a falling climber can be equally hazardous to the spotter. The general rule for highballs (and all bouldering for that matter) is to ensure that the falling climber lands on the pads and stays on the pads after impact. Spotting might look less like controlling and guiding the fall and more like giving the falling climber a shove to keep them on the pads. The spotter(s) should also protect the head and neck from striking bare ground, rocks, etc.

In his report to *ANAC*, Korpics continued:

We could have used more pads to cover the drop zone and thinner pads to cover gaps between pads. This accident may also have been prevented by assertive spotting—a strong shove from one of the spotters would have landed me on the pads. That possibility was negated because I had instructed my spotters to stand clear if I fell from above the crux.

Confidence should not lead to complacency. I'd been climbing a lot and climbing well, including numerous highballs prior to the accident, so I'd let my guard down. I do not blame the spotters, as I had given them specific instructions. I had placed the pads, I chose to climb despite knowing more pads would be better, and the injury was my fault. *(Sources: Pete Korpics, MountainProject.com, and the Editors.)*

TENNESSEE

GROUND FALL | Missed Clip

Foster Falls, The Left Bunker

On the second day of a weekend trip to Foster Falls, Randall Ladd (34) and I, Brian West (28), decided to work on our project, Eclipse (5.12c/d). The route is very steep, with mostly clean air falls and no overhead hazard. I decided not to wear a helmet, though I almost always wear one.

At the bottom of the route, the ground rises and follows the wall. This means that if you fall clipping the second or third (or even fourth) bolt, there's a chance of hitting the ground. After the third or fourth bolt, it's all good.

We stick-clipped the first two bolts. I climbed through the crux, which is just past the second bolt, and then moved to the good hold used to clip the third. I pulled up some rope but fell before getting the rope in the draw. I felt secure and I'm not sure what made me slip. I do not remember falling, but I was told I landed with my body nearly horizontal. The second bolt caught me, but the rope stretched and let me hit the ground. My upper back impacted first, and I was pulled up by the rebounding rope and left hanging a few inches above the ground. Randall lowered me; I was unconscious and had seizure-like convulsions.

After a few minutes, I woke up. I had a significant cut on the back of my head. The EMTs arrived, bandaged my head, and asked if I was able to walk to the parking lot. I decided to try and made it without much trouble. A friend drove me to the ER. I had a CT scan and was stapled, gauzed, and told my injuries required no further attention.

Everything about Eclipse (5.12c/d) is classic, except for the third clip. In February 2024, Brian West fell from near this spot, ending up in the hospital—he was not wearing a helmet. Here we see the helmeted West on an earlier attempt. He has the second bolt clipped. The third bolt is up and to the right of his head. *Brian West*

ANALYSIS

While a helmet wouldn't have kept me from hitting the ground, it would have protected my head. I probably would have walked away with bruised shoulders, a bruised back...and a bruised ego. I won't make that mistake again.

I could have avoided the ground fall had I asked for some tension to take a controlled fall rather than attempting the clip. Pre-clipping the third bolt with a stick-clip or while clipped in direct to the second was another option. Pulling up slack to clip the second or third draw is often a "no fall" situation that applies to many routes. Personally, if I'm not sure about a clip, I'll hang or take the whip. In this case, I felt secure. Apparently, I wasn't.

My accident was a convergence of several things going wrong at once. Climbers and belayers should be aware of how much slack is out, especially close to the ground. Climbers should not pull excessive rope to clip. Belayers should limit slack in the system and feed just enough to clip and nothing more. *(Source: Brian West.)*

The Kor-Ingalls Route on Castleton Tower climbs the shaded cracks on the right side of the formation. First climbed in 1961 by Layton Kor and Huntley Ingalls, it is included in Steve Roper and Allen Steck's *Fifty Classic Climbs of North America*. Modern climbers find that several "old-school" sections are tricky and hard to protect. *Ronald J Scott—Wikimedia*

UTAH

PROTECTION PULLED OUT

Moab, Castleton Tower

On the morning of October 26, Grand County Search and Rescue received a call for help from a climber (mid-40s) who had sustained an open lower leg fracture. The climbing team was at the beginning of the second pitch of the Kor-Ingalls Route (4 pitches, 5.9+) on Castleton Tower. Both EMS and SAR responded with helicopter support to the area. Rescuers climbed up, administered care, and packaged the patient—who was hauled off the route, then flown to the hospital.

Rescuers learned that this team had planned to climb the North Chimney (5.9) that day but had found a long line of climbers in front of them. Instead of waiting, they pivoted to the Kor-Ingalls. The second pitch—referred to as "honest 5.8" on Mountain Project—has a 40-foot section of sustained and slippery fist-sized crack that for most climbers requires multiple number 4-sized Camalots for protection. This climbing team had only one number 4 cam but thought they might be okay using a number 3 instead. After climbing the first pitch without incident, the climber had started up the second. Finding the fist crack longer and harder than expected, he placed the number3, clipped it, and grabbed it, hoping to downclimb to his number 4. The tipped-out number3 cam pulled out and he fell all the way to a ledge, breaking his leg.

ANALYSIS

Crowds are an unfortunate reality in climbing. This team of experienced climbers had knowledge of an alternate route but did not bring the proper equipment for both routes. When the climber realized that the difficulty exceeded his expectations, he did not have adequate protection below him. His partner was able to administer first aid and rescuers were able to access him in a timely manner, but it is always a good idea to be proficient at self-rescue in these remote areas. Finally, it's a good idea to thoroughly research one's intended route. *(Source: Grand County Search and Rescue.)*

ANCHOR FAILURE

Moab Area, River Road

On the evening of April 21, Grand County Search and Rescue was notified of an overdue male climber (approximate age 25). At 3 p.m., the subject had described to co-workers his plan to retrieve a stuck rope by himself; he did not return to work. The subject's car was found at the parking area for the Sorcerer's Apprentice formation along River Road.

The subject had posted on the "Moab Rock Climbers" Facebook group earlier that day, agreeing to retrieve a stuck rope from the Sorcerer's Apprentice Left route (2 pitches, 5.11c). Another party had posted a request for help because they were leaving town and couldn't retrieve the rope themselves. The subject simply responded "got it" to the post but did not request any additional information.

Sorcerer's Apprentice Left (5.11c) climbs two pitches up the shaded, left-facing corner. A lone climber fell to his death in spring of 2024 while retrieving a stuck rappel rope. *Eric Dixon*

The left side of the Sorcerer's Apprentice is also the standard rappel route for both routes on the formation. A double-rope rappel descends the long first pitch (5.10+) of Sorcerer's Apprentice Left. Presumably, the rappel rope got stuck partway down from the top of the pitch when pulled by the other climbing team the previous day.

The subject was found deceased at the base of the formation. He was rigged to ascend; the rope still ran through a Grigri clipped to the belay loop of his harness and through a Micro Traxion (with attached foot loop) above the Grigri. He was trailing a second climbing rope with him but had no additional climbing gear. It appears the subject fell about 70 feet, sustaining fatal injuries. Likely he was ascending the stuck rope when it dislodged from whatever was holding it in place.

ANALYSIS

It is clear that the rope was not securely attached despite holding the climber's body weight for some time. Never trust your life to a rope without knowing it is securely anchored. A safer alternative would have been to re-lead the pitch while placing gear. The subject must have known/assumed that the stuck rope was somehow jammed in the bolt anchor at the top of the pitch as he did not have any gear on his harness to build a retreat anchor, nor to protect his progress up whatever might have remained of the pitch. *(Sources: Grand County Search and Rescue and the Editors.)*

WASHINGTON

FALL ON ROCK

North Cascades National Park, Thornton Peak

On August 3 at approximately 2:40 p.m., the Whatcom County Sheriff's Office notified North Cascades National Park climbing rangers of a potential rescue situation on Thornton Peak. Initial information was that a 36-year-old female had a lower leg that was said to be both limp and bleeding. Given the possibility of uncontrolled bleeding and a potential threat to the limb, NPS incident command launched a helicopter for a possible short-haul evacuation. A ground-based rescue would require five miles of hiking on trail followed by two additional miles off-trail, with more than 4,000 feet of elevation gain. Additionally, accessing the injured climber would involve technical climbing and possible rockfall.

The NPS helicopter was already in the vicinity attending to an unrelated operation. The incident commander briefed the helicopter crew at 2:45 p.m. Following this briefing, the crew completed a pre-mission risk assessment and launched for flight. At 3:15 p.m. Skagit County dispatch received another distress call relaying that the patient's leg had continued to bleed and that they were applying a tourniquet. At 3:21 p.m., the helicopter located the patient and identified a nearby landing site. The rescue team descended and the rangers reported that the bleeding remained uncontrolled. Concurrently, the crew began packaging the patient. Following a short-haul operation, the patient was transferred to an air ambulance staged in Marblemount, Washington.

ANALYSIS

In this incident, the climbing party did what they could for a potentially life/limb-threatening injury. An open fracture, coupled with the inability to control bleeding, could have resulted in a far worse outcome. The extremely efficient response time was due in large part to the fact that a helicopter, shared by two other national parks, happened to already be close by. In this incident, many favorable variables resulted in a timely evacuation of a critical patient. This includes the climbers having adequate communication to summon rescue and basic first-aid skills. *(Source: North Cascades National Park Climbing Rangers.)*

FALL FROM ANCHOR | Rappel Ring Detached from Slings

North Cascades, Cutthroat Peak

On April 28, Thomas Gilbert and Philip Bond were descending the Cauthorn-Wilson Route on Cutthroat Peak in the North Cascades. The route is a seasonal ice climb (7 pitches, WI4). At approximately 8 p.m., a rappel failure caused Bond to fall 400 feet, taking the ropes with him. He fell 120 feet down WI3+ terrain, then another 260 feet down steep snow. He survived and came to rest in deep snow at approximately 7,200 feet elevation. Gilbert was left at the rappel station with no ropes and no way of safely downclimbing. Both climbers had a Garmin inReach and were able to initiate an SOS.

Chelan County Mountain Rescue (CCMR) was notified at approximately 10 p.m., and a team of three was assembled. The weather was deteriorating, so time was critical. They decided to move through the night to reach the location. CCMR personnel left Wenatchee around 11:40 p.m. and were hiking toward the climbers at 2:45 a.m. on April 29. The CCMR team was joined by two members of Okanogan County Search and Rescue (OCSAR). They arrived at Bond's location at 5 a.m.

More members of OCSAR and CCMR were dispatched, and Naval Air Station Whidbey Island (NASWI) was requested to prepare for a helicopter extraction. Two members of CCMR climbed to Gilbert, reaching him at 7 a.m. The team below stabilized Bond's injuries and warmed him using sleeping bags, "chem kits," food, water, and shelter. The two CCMR climbers lowered Gilbert to the other team members. Around 10:20 a.m., the weather cleared enough to allow NASWI to hoist out the stricken climbers. All rescuers were able to hike out.

Thomas Gilbert (yellow circle) is showered by spindrift at the belay/rappel station on the Cauthorn-Wilson Route on Cutthroat Peak. He was stranded overnight one pitch above the ground after his partner fell while rappelling, taking the ropes with him. *CCMR*

ANALYSIS

A failure at the anchor caused Bond to fall almost as soon as he weighted the rappel ropes. The anchor consisted of three pitons connected by a 6mm cord. Attached to an equalized point on that cord was a rappel ring. The climbers were using twin ropes, and the ropes were threaded through the rappel ring. There did not appear to be any cord or gear failure at the anchor itself and the rappel ring was still threaded by the ropes that fell with Bond. There was no evidence of broken slings or cordage.

It is believed the rappel ring was not tied directly to the anchor cord but was girth-hitched to the cord. The hypothesis is that the climbers grabbed the "wrong side" of the rappel ring, which caused it to rotate and detach itself. *(See the graphic below that shows how this might occur.)* It is believed that the cord was lightly frozen

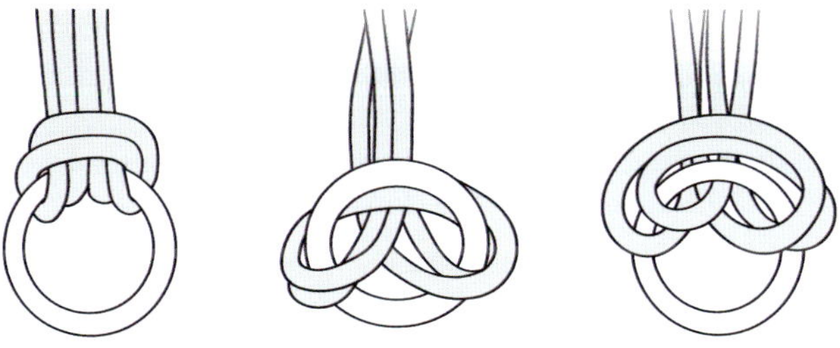

Left: A rappel ring girth-hitched with anchor cord. Middle: If the girth hitch is too loose, the cord may slip down the sides, exposing the "top" of the ring. Right: If a rappel rope is threaded through the top of the ring and weighted, the ring may flip and detach from the hitched cord. *Foster Denney*

and the climbers, who were in a hurry to get down, did not notice that the girth hitch had "flipped" (*see previous page*) when they were feeding their ropes.

We have noticed that girth-hitching anchors is becoming increasingly common in our area, and the above illustrates this lesser-known hazard. Climbers should properly inspect anchors to ensure they are sound. More accidents are occurring from bad rappel slings. We recommend cutting off old cord and slings. Use a locking carabiner or "cheapskate locker" in place of rappel rings (*see page 18*). Pear-shaped carabiners have less of a chance of "rolling" in the cord than rappel rings.

Also, the rappel should always be properly weight-tested before one detaches their personal anchor system. *(Sources: Chelan County Mountain Rescue, Okanogan County SAR, and the Editors.)*

LEADER FALL | Arm Tangled in Rope

Leavenworth, Rattlesnake Rock

My name is Emma, and on May 27, I was leading up Tubbing at Der Ritterhoff (5.11a sport) for a second time when I had an unusual accident. As I was approaching the roof section of the climb, I went up to make a clip. Then I remembered that I needed to position myself farther left, so I stepped back down. When I moved up again to climb through the roof, I fell about 15 or 20 feet. The fall itself was clean and safe, but I had not realized that while backing off earlier, a loop of rope had fallen over my right arm. In the fall, the loop cinched around my upper arm. The force of the fall transected the muscles in that area, causing a complete tear through the biceps muscle.

Two other climbers helped my partner set up a rope to lower me down the steepest portion of the approach trail. We drove to the ER in Leavenworth, and I had surgery two weeks later to repair the muscles.

ANALYSIS

I have always been warned about letting the rope run behind my legs, but I had not thought about how it could wrap around my arm. It was also a fairly warm day and my second time on the route; I had intended to top-rope it, but decided to try and lead it clean, though I was tired. This might have caused my inattention to the position of the rope around my arm. The sun angle also prevented my belayer from seeing the loop of rope and alerting me about it.

Rope awareness is the responsibility of the person climbing, but I am still thinking about how this might have been mitigated. *(Sources: Emma Chabal and Dylan Albrecht.)*

AVALANCHE AND ROCKFALL | Stranded

Mt. Rainier, Liberty Ridge

At 1:30 p.m. on June 6, Mt. Rainier climbing rangers were notified about a satellite SOS activation on Liberty Ridge. The incident commander was able to directly message two climbers, who were stranded at 9,700 feet. Rockfall had hit one climber in the head. A helicopter was dispatched with two rangers, and during the reconnaissance flight, the stranded pair was located. Plans were formulated for a short-haul rescue. A team was inserted on the ridge and extricated the distressed climbers. Both were taken to Camp Schurman and on to a hospital.

Interviews revealed that the two climbers from Colorado had set off at 12:30 a.m.

to climb Liberty Ridge. At 5:30 a.m., they began the technical section of the route. June 6 was one of the first days of clear skies and warm temperatures following several weeks of snowfall. The forecasted freezing level was at 13,000 feet. The climbers reported "30 to 40 avalanches throughout the day, one every eight minutes before the accident."

The climbers had discussed turning around but were unsure if they could find anchors to rappel, given the vast sections of rock. At 11 a.m., they turned around as they approached Thumb Rock (11,000 feet). The injured climber reported that a 35-pound rock had fallen 200 feet, striking him on the upper back and neck. Rangers found no obvious signs of trauma during patient assessment.

ANALYSIS

A Mt. Rainier National Park climbing ranger reported speaking with this party on June 5. The ranger highlighted the need for conservative decision making following the recent series of storms and advised a different route or, at the minimum, observing their proposed route during daylight hours before an attempt. The ranger warned that Liberty Ridge is very avalanche-prone following snowfall. The climbers had also contacted a local guiding company on June 5 to acquire conditions information. During that call, a senior mountain guide suggested that the Coloradans should stay off Liberty Ridge, given the weather and route conditions.

The climbers had been advised to adopt a self-sufficient mindset and prepare for self-rescue. They reported that an avalanche had destroyed the snow bridge across the bergschrund that they crossed on the morning of their ill-fated attempt. They said that rappelling into and climbing out of the bergschrund was the only option for descent and claimed that this prevented retreat. They further claimed that self-rescue would have required them to "push for the summit."

While the ambition to climb a major technical route is admirable, climbers must be mindful when conditions are bad. Patience is prudent on a climb like Liberty Ridge. Having the skills, experience, and equipment for retreat is mandatory. In this instance, the ability to rappel into a crevasse and climb out the other side would have negated the need for a rescue that endangered rescuers.

An emergency satellite communication device should not be a default option when choosing to do a dangerous ascent. In this case, rapid response was only made possible because of favorable flying conditions. Climbers should not assume that ground or air rescue will be possible, much less prompt. Route selection should be based on a climbing team's ability and fitness level, plus an experienced assessment of conditions and the forecast. The life you risk may not just be your own (*see Danger Zones in ANAC 2014*). *(Source: Mt. Rainier Climbing Rangers.)*

FALL ON SNOW | Crampon Snag While Fleeing Falling Serac

Mt. Rainier, Emmons Glacier

On June 29, I (male, 35) and two partners (both male, 40 and 36) were descending the Emmons Glacier after a summit attempt. A little after 7 a.m., a serac collapsed higher on the mountain. We were around the 11,000-foot level, near the top of the "Corridor" feature, on a 25° to 30° slope. We soon saw tumbling blocks of ice and snow crest the slope above us; the debris was initially fridge-sized and broke into smaller pieces. I was at the back of the rope team and had the least time to react. I ran to avoid being hit, and in doing so, I caught my left crampon on my right leg.

I fell and ended up in a self-arrest position, with my head facing uphill, as the debris sped by. My right leg/knee was twisted in the fall. I was not injured by the small pieces of falling serac debris. My two partners also moved to avoid the falling debris and were not hit.

We moved about a hundred feet to the side of the debris fall line. I knew that my right leg/knee was injured and had to crawl. My partners probed for crevasses and dug a small platform with a shovel.

Once we were in a safe position, my partners assessed my injuries and determined I was not able to walk down the glacier to Camp Schurman, where we had camped the previous day. We had sufficient gear to improvise a rescue sled/drag-bag, but as the most experienced member of the team, I felt it was safer and more efficient to request assistance. (We had sufficient gear for an extended bivy.) Though we could see Camp Schurman (where the rangers were), we did not have cell reception, so we activated an inReach.

Fortunately, the weather was warm and my pain level was not too bad. The rangers were notified at 8:30 a.m. and a plan was developed. Two climbing rangers left Camp Schurman on foot to coordinate a helicopter rescue—or lower me to camp in the event that weather prevented helicopter extraction. They requested we dig a platform and anchor ourselves. We worked to make our platform larger, placed a picket as an anchor, and prepared our gear and packs.

The rangers on foot arrived at 10:40 a.m. Then the helicopter arrived. The climbing rangers assessed my injuries and our platform and asked my partners to dig a second platform and anchor. They splinted my leg, and I was short-hauled at 11 a.m. to Camp Schurman. Shortly after we left, dense clouds moved in, which may have prevented a helicopter rescue. I was thankful to have been rescued quickly and am grateful to the Rainier climbing rangers, the helicopter crew, and Greenwater Fire and Rescue.

I was diagnosed with a tibial plateau compression fracture. There were some complications, but I am expected to make a full recovery.

ANALYSIS

We were on the least objectively hazardous route to the summit of Mt. Rainier, yet we were still exposed to falling debris. The weather was not particularly warm overnight (11,000-foot freezing level). It was also forecasted to get cooler on the morning of the accident, with the freezing level dropping to 10,000 feet. The serac fall occurred after the sun had warmed the mountain, but we were the earliest group to begin descending on that day.

I believe we made the right call to request help. It was good that I got off the mountain before bad weather came in. I do not regret running from the falling serac debris, as it could have been very serious had I been struck by falling debris.

I was grateful we had our Wilderness First Responder training, were well prepared with food and clothing to wait for help, and had two-way messaging. When we chose to enter complex, glaciated terrain, we accepted a certain level of risk and took all possible precautions. *(Source: Anonymous.)*

UNFINISHED KNOT

Vantage, Millennium Wall

On November 23, I (Randy Bracht) was climbing with friends in the Frenchman Coulee area near Vantage, Washington. These desert cliffs are a popular cragging destination for climbers from around the Pacific Northwest.

We were at Millennium Wall, which mostly consists of single-pitch bolted sport climbs ranging up to 60 feet in height. I was leading a route called Heel Higher Crescent (10a). I was 35 feet off the deck and about to clip the fourth bolt when I noticed my rewoven figure-8 knot dangling about a foot below my harness.

"Whaaaat?" I thought, momentarily confused. "Why does that look so weird?"

I realized that my figure-8 knot had never been rewoven. On the ground, I got engaged in a conversation with my belayer. In my distracted state, I forgot to finish tying the knot. I also forgot to check it myself and forgot to do a partner check with my belayer. This felt monumentally stupid for a guy who has been climbing for over 30 years without suffering any serious accidents...so far.

Fortunately, the tail end of the rope had not slipped out of the leg and waist loops on my harness and I was positioned at a bolt that I could quickly clip with my anchor sling. Dangling there, I finished tying my rewoven figure-8 and completed the route without incident.

In recent years, Frenchman Coulee, a.k.a. Vantage, has emerged as a destination climbing area, with sport routes and superb crack climbs on columnar basalt. Pictured here is a popular area known as the Feathers. The density of routes and ease of access can make for a very social—and distracting—environment. *Walter Siegmund—Wikimedia*

ANALYSIS

No harm, no foul, whether by providence or sheer dumb luck, right? I could let this sobering episode slip by without public notice and personal embarrassment. But, if you'll allow a religious analogy, it's good to confess your sin before the congregation, with the hope of saving another soul.

You've heard this before and from better people than me, but I'll repeat it: Don't allow yourself to be distracted while tying in. At the gym, at the crag, in the mountains. Finish that lifesaving knot. Do partner checks, but don't expect your partner/belayer to ask to look at it before leaving the ground. INSIST that they look at it. Belayers, do likewise. *(Source: Randy Bracht.)*

Blacktail Butte (foreground), the Middle Teton (left center), and the Grand Teton (highest peak) all saw plenty of climbers and several accidents in 2024. ***Sam Beebe—Wikimedia***

WYOMING

FALL ON ROCK

Grand Teton National Park, Middle Teton, Southwest Couloir

On July 24, a 22-year-old female climber fell on steep snow while descending the Southwest Couloir Route on the Middle Teton (12,809 feet). The fall occurred while the climber was traveling on a shortcut to avoid the usual path to the saddle below and thereby make an early entry into the upper South Fork of Garnet Canyon. The reporting party relayed that the patient had a "serious" hip injury and was unable to walk. The climber was short-hauled by helicopter to an awaiting ambulance and taken to the hospital.

Several weeks later (August 17) on the same shortcut, a 21-year-old female lost her footing and slid into a moat near the exit of the Middle Teton's Southwest Couloir and the saddle between the South and Middle Tetons. Two climbing rangers were inserted via helicopter, and after assessing the patient, they treated significant and bleeding head lacerations. She and one rescuer were short-hauled out. She was then transferred to ambulance personnel, but despite the severity of her injuries, she refused further medical treatment.

ANALYSIS

Both of these events illustrate an almost annual summer occurrence in the Tetons in which climbing rangers respond to accidents in this area (*see ANAC 2024 and ANAC 2016*). Climbers are advised that although it is shorter, the shortcut terrain is deceptively steep and often holds snow underfoot. The longer, gentler route descending to the true saddle between the South and Middle Tetons is often more efficient. *(Source: Grand Teton National Park Search and Rescue Report.)*

FALL ON ROCK | Loose Rock

Grand Teton National Park, Grand Teton

On August 21, Jim Dahle and Christian Feinauer embarked on a one-day ascent of the North Face of the Grand Teton (12 pitches, 5.8). The forecast called for fine weather, although winds were likely to pick up in the afternoon. The team rapidly progressed up the glacier and crossed two crevasses before reaching the bergschrund. Jim led across the bergschrund, and Christian led the second pitch, eventually belaying on a one-by-five-foot ledge. Jim arrived and took over the lead. After about 20 feet of 4th class, he reached a steep, shallow dihedral. He placed four pieces as he moved up, the last being a small cam in questionable rock.

About eight feet above the small cam, all of his holds were loose. The climbing looked easier and more solid about six feet up and to the right. Jim reached for a large hold, but it pulled off. As he fell, the small cam pulled, sending him for a 30- to 35-foot fall into broken 4th-class terrain. He struck the right side of his face, his right shoulder, and his left hand. He was left hanging upside down 15 feet above and to the right of his belayer.

This photo was taken after a 30-plus-foot leader fall low on the North Face of the Grand Teton. The leader's high point is visible (blue X), as is the failed cam placement (red arrow). The fall ended at the yellow arrow. ***Christian Feinauer***

Jim was unresponsive and leaking blood and cerebrospinal fluid (CSF) from his face. The team's inReach was in his pack. After several minutes, Christian tied off the fallen climber and soloed over. He secured himself and assessed his partner. Jim regained consciousness after ten minutes but was perseverating—repeatedly asking the same questions. Christian returned to the belay and coached Jim to the anchor. Jim's right eye was swollen shut, he had large forehead lacerations, and CSF dripped from his nose. His mental state was severely altered. Self-rescue was not an option.

Christian layered his partner with all available clothes. He dialed 911 and was eventually transferred to the Jenny Lake Rangers. Coincidentally, the rangers were gathered for helicopter rescue training. They rapidly launched a rescue and flew to the scene to scope out the situation. The stranded team was located at a spot where direct insertion and short-haul were viable.

The pair was extricated and Jim was flown to the regional medical center. His injuries included a severe concussion, multiple facial fractures, a significant CSF leak, a wrist fracture, right AC separation, fractured ribs, and a C7 spine fracture. He's had a near complete functional recovery and was able to resume climbing six months later.

ANALYSIS

Both climbers were very experienced and had partnered on dozens of successful alpine rock routes. Given their experience and preparation, the North Face of the Grand was well within their ability.

The severity of the accident came down to a loose hold, leading to a bad fall in a bad location. In retrospect, Jim might have downclimbed to more stable rock. Climbers should also remember that "psychological protection" in loose rock should not encourage the leader to continue upward. If one is not comfortable with a runout, then retreat and reassessment are in order. Abandoning the route is also an option.

The NPS report summed up that, despite being in a very inaccessible location, the rescue was efficient: "The time from initial 911 notification to patient extraction was two hours and five minutes. Multiple factors—including available rescuers, a helicopter in proximity, and favorable weather—all fell into place. Ultimately, the preparedness of the climbing partners to assess, stabilize, and notify authorities won the day." *(Sources: Dr. Jim Dahle and Grand Teton National Park Search and Rescue.)*

FALL ON ROCK | Unanchored Belayer

Grand Teton National Park, Grand Teton

On the afternoon of July 16, a 72-year-old male fell while leading on the Upper Exum Ridge of the Grand Teton. Luckily, he landed on the ledge from which he was being belayed. This climber sustained significant injuries and was having difficulty breathing. Due to the severity of his condition, rescuers were short-hauled directly to the scene for patient extraction. Climbing rangers secured the climber in a litter and short-hauled him to Lupine Meadows. The patient was transferred to an ambulance and on to the local hospital. The partner and a second rescuer also were short-hauled to the valley.

ANALYSIS

This group was moving very slowly. They began the technical climbing section of the route well after all guided and private parties were back in camp or descending to the trailhead. The injured climber had not placed any protection, nor was his belayer anchored to the wall. If the belay ledge had not arrested his fall, both climbers likely would have fallen to their deaths.

There are several basic yet important lessons here. First, teams should consistently assess their progress and turn around when significantly behind schedule or when conditions dramatically take a turn for the worst. Second, if you are the leader, protect yourself and your partner by placing gear. Finally, if you are the belayer, protect your team by placing an anchor. *(Source: Grand Teton National Park Search and Rescue Report.)*

HIGH ALTITUDE ILLNESS

Grand Teton National Park, Lower Saddle and Garnet Canyon

On July 17, a 22-year-old female climber was unable to descend under her own power from the Lower Saddle (11,600 feet). The primary cause of her nonambulatory status

With the Middle Teton (center right) dominating the skyline, Garnet Canyon presents a beautiful and relatively low-altitude (9,280 feet) vista. Still, without proper acclimatization, climbers can easily suffer high altitude illness here, as in the incident on the facing page. ***NPS—Wikimedia***

was fatigue brought on by high altitude illness (HAI). Climbing rangers assessed and treated the patient and allowed her to rest. Following these interventions, the climber was able to continue her descent approximately eight hours later without incident.

A week later, on July 24, a 66-year-old female was evacuated by helicopter from Garnet Meadows (9,280 feet) in Garnet Canyon. This guided client was assessed by both her guides and NPS rangers, who concluded this was likely HAI. After helicopter transport to Lupine Meadows, the sick patient was transferred to an ambulance and taken to the local hospital for further observation.

ANALYSIS

Although less common in the Teton Range than on Mt. McKinley, Mt. Rainier, and other summits, HAI affects some climbers in the range every climbing season. These two incidents highlight the need to monitor oneself and also one's climbing partners for signs and symptoms of HAI. A safe maxim is to discontinue ascent whenever the possibility exists. Refer to the 2024 edition of *ANAC* for a comprehensive write-up on the assessment, treatment, and prevention of HAI. *(Source: Grand Teton National Park Search and Rescue Report.)*

RAPPEL ANCHOR FAILURE | Old Webbing

Grand Teton National Park, Middle Teton, Glacier Route

On July 3, two male climbers summited the Middle Teton via the Northwest Couloir Route. As the weather deteriorated and winds increased, the climbers elected to descend the Middle Teton Glacier Route (Grade III 5.4 AI2+) instead of the standard 3rd-class Southwest Couloir. The weather was cloudy with temperatures near 40°F, winds between 20 and 30 mph, and intermittent snow/rain and scattered thunderstorms.

The climbers encountered steep terrain 100 feet below the summit and decided to rappel. They completed two 60-meter rappels from anchors they placed. The climbers then found a fixed anchor that consisted of two pieces of webbing slung around a rock. They inspected the webbing and placed a camming device as a backup. The cam was not tensioned to the slings, so the webbing remained isolated as they bounce-tested the anchor. They deemed the anchor adequate.

The first climber rappelled 175 feet to a snowfield. He detached from the rope and began searching for the next anchor. Shortly after this, the second climber (age 60) removed the backup cam and began rappelling. The webbing broke shortly after he began the rappel and he fell approximately 250 feet over rock, snow, and ice before landing on a ledge at 12,200 feet.

His partner descended, anchored the fallen climber, and then assessed his injuries. The patient remained awake and oriented but was nonambulatory due to a leg injury. He was ultimately diagnosed with a shoulder dislocation with three associated minor fractures, fractures of C1 and C2 vertebrae, and a fractured tibia. The uninjured climber contacted SAR at 3:54 p.m., and a helicopter was requested.

At 4:36 p.m., three climbing rangers were flown in to assess the accident site. High winds prevented a short-haul rescue, and instead two rangers were dropped at the Lower Saddle for a ground rescue. Six additional rangers were shuttled to the Lower Saddle. The first two rangers climbed the North Ridge of the Middle Teton in poor conditions. They advised subsequent teams to approach via the Glacier Route. The six additional rangers, equipped with gear to perform a technical ground rescue, descended to the Middle Teton Glacier and climbed toward the injured climber.

At 7:20 p.m., the first climbing ranger arrived on scene. At 7:45 p.m., rangers reported favorable winds, and at 8:10 p.m., the patient and a ranger were short-hauled off the mountain.

ANALYSIS

The primary lesson here is the importance of using sound rappel anchors. Even with inspection, gear found in the field is suspect. Erring on the side of caution and building one's own anchors is a reasonable way to minimize this risk. The patient later said that in his 52 years of climbing, he always placed his own anchors. The exception on this one day was after poor weather pushed them to make haste into unfamiliar terrain. A quick and inexpensive solution for building—or in this case reinforcing—a sling anchor is to carry a small knife, some cord, and a "cheapskate locker" (*see page 17*). *(Source: Grand Teton National Park Search and Rescue Report.)*

ROCKFALL

Grand Teton National Park, Upper Blacktail Butte

On the afternoon of May 30, Jenna Jones (18) was gearing up at the base of a sport crag when she was struck in the head by a falling rock. Jenna sent the following report to *ANAC*:

While on a Teton trip with my boyfriend, "A," we decided to do a quick climb at Upper Blacktail Butte. Neither of us had been there before, and we decided on a 5.9 route after some internet research. After hiking to the base, "A" went to the top of the cliff to set up a top-rope. I had a wonderful view of the Tetons as I was putting my harness on; my helmet wasn't even out of the bag yet. That is all I remember, because at that point I was struck in the head by a boulder that had fallen from the top of the 60-foot cliff. "A" had a misstep while setting up the top-rope and dislodged the rock.

I regained consciousness about five minutes later. "A" was making a tourniquet out of his T-shirt. I felt no pain due to adrenaline and shock. I went unconscious again and woke up six hours later in the Idaho Falls ER. A doctor was giving me lidocaine shots prior to receiving stitches and staples. Pain set in quickly when my consciousness returned. I was told I needed brain surgery. I was also unable to have food or water until 2 a.m., when it was decided that I no longer needed the surgery. After two nights in the ICU, I was cleared to go home. A long road of recovery lay ahead of me.

ANALYSIS

I believe everyone at the base should be cautious of loose rock falling from the top. Those who are above should take extreme caution to not dislodge rocks from the top of the cliff. I would have had my helmet on within three minutes had the rock not fallen, since I was getting all my gear on. I think it is safe to say helmets should be put on first when reaching the climb site. *(Source: Jenna Jones.)*

**Editor's Note:* There have been at least four incidents in the last few years of climbers being struck by falling rock while at the base of a climb. Most of these accidents ended in fatalities, and as terrible as Jenna's accident was, she can count herself as fortunate.

LEADER FALL ON ROCK

Devils Tower, Durrance Area

We drove up to Devils Tower and on August 31, with nobody behind us, we took our time racking up for the Durrance Route (6 pitches, 5.7+). Person 2 (male, 41) led the approach pitch. Person 1 (male, 23) then started up the first real pitch (the Leaning Column), climbing steadily. As he started toward the top of the column about 70 feet up, his foot popped off and he fell. Person 1 impacted the ledge below with both feet.

Person 1 had Wilderness First Responder experience, and after waiting several minutes he did a self-evaluation. His feet were bruised but had full movement and did not feel broken. The bolts for the top of the pitch were quite close, so he continued. When he arrived at the belay, everything still appeared normal, so he

A climber injured his leg on the first pitch of the Durrance Route (just right of the sun/shade line in the middle of this photo). Though his partner offered to bail, the climber considered the time they had invested in the trip and decided to continue to the top. *w_lemay—Wikimedia*

continued, linking that first pitch with the next.

Person 1 climbed the next three pitches, but slowly realized his knee could not be weighted. By the time he led to the top, Person 1 was unable to weight the knee on flat ground. The two climbers rappelled, and Person 1 limped and butt-scooted down the trail. Person 1 believes that he smashed his knee into the wall while falling; this dislocated his kneecap, which caused a osteochondral fracture of the femur.

ANALYSIS

Person 1 could have placed more protection. Person 2 also may have been overconfident in his partner's ability and gave an unnecessarily loose belay. Being close to the ledge, Person 1 likely would have decked regardless, but some of the force might have been absorbed had he had a tighter belay.

Person 1 also did not recognize that a serious injury might have occurred and decided to continue climbing. Fortunately, the injury was a deep bone bruise that healed without pins or a cast. The desire to summit might have played a role in this accident, as the team had driven seven hours to climb the route. *(Source: Person 1.)*

FATAL RAPPEL FALL

Devils Tower

On September 22, a rock climber named Stewart Phillip Porter (21) died from injuries sustained during a fall at Devils Tower National Monument. The accident occurred shortly before 8 p.m. Devils Tower Law Enforcement was informed, and responding staff found the injured party and their climbing partner at around 8:40 p.m. Porter was pronounced dead on scene by paramedics.

Porter and his partner had summited and were rappelling the second pitch of El Cracko Diablo when Porter fell. His partner was stranded and was later rescued from the wall, with help from Devils Tower Lodge Climbing Guides and Buck Wild Climbing Guides.

ANALYSIS

According to comments on the accident that appeared on MountainProject.com, Porter had cut his 70-meter rope down to 66 meters and apparently there was no middle mark. At the end of the rappel, the rope ends were uneven. He rappelled off the short end, taking the rope with him when he fell.

The day before, Porter had climbed a route called Soler and did the El Cracko Diablo rappel descent. He then climbed El Cracko, posting on Mountain Project, "After Soler, rapped this [El Cracko Diablo] with a 66m in three raps, then climbed this to the top." It is not known which route he climbed prior to his death on the rappel descent.

As the Park Service states: "Over the 100 plus year climbing history at the Tower, there have only been seven climbing deaths. The majority of climbing accidents and deaths on the Tower occur during the rappel. The National Park Service does not maintain anchors—inspect all anchors and back them up if necessary. Ensure you know the location of your rappel route before you begin. Start rappels over the nose of columns to prevent ropes from jamming in cracks. Avoid knocking loose rock onto climbers below. Many rappels require two ropes; know the distance of your planned rappel before beginning." *(Sources: NPS and MountainProject.com.)*

Mt. Robson is majestic when viewed from afar. The Wishbone Arête traverses the lower face to gain the sharp ridge diagonaling up and left to the summit. In August 2024, a trio of climbers was nearing the top when one of their party fell. ***Gopi.Perumal—Wikimedia***

CANADA

FATAL FALL ON ROCK | Climbing Unroped

British Columbia, Mt. Robson

On August 31, two climbers near the summit of Mt. Robson (12,972 feet) requested a rescue. They reported that a third member (male, 25) had fallen off the mountain.

The party had ascended the Wishbone Arête route (IV 5.6) and was 350 meters from the summit. It had snowed the night before the accident, which may have been a contributing factor in the fall. The deceased climber had been unroped when he fell. The two survivors spent the night near the summit before being flown off by Parks Canada SAR.

The upper half of the south face of Mt. Robson, seen from a rescue helicopter. The deceased climber fell from the yellow X and was later found on a ledge 750 meters below (yellow rectangle). ***Parks Canada***

ANALYSIS

The Wishbone Arête is an exceptionally long and serious climb on Mt. Robson, the highest peak in the Canadian Rockies. Though featured in *Fifty Classic Climbs of North America*, it has been called "the worst route in Canada." This moniker is derived from poor rock quality, meandering climbing, and the fact that much of the route involves 3rd- and 4th-class terrain, often tackled unroped. Terrain like this exposes climbers to serious fall potential and protection is poor to nonexistent. In a full report on this tragic attempt (linked to at the *ANAC* website), one of the surviving climbers wrote, "There is just no safe way to climb it [Wishbone Arête].... If you are considering climbing Mt. Robson, find another route." *(Sources: The climbers, Parks Canada, and CascadeClimbers.com.)*

LEADER FALL ON ICE | Insecure Tool Placements

Alberta, Jasper National Park, Tangle Ridge

On December 27, three climbers were attempting the Rick Blak Memorial Route (WI5), a 30-meter ice climb in Jasper National Park. The leader was nearing the top of the pitch when her ice tools popped, resulting in a ten meter fall caught by a 13-centimeter ice screw. During the fall, her crampon caught on the ice and was ripped from her boot. The resulting force broke her lower leg.

The team lowered the injured climber and moved her to an open area away from the cliffs. Using a VHF radio, the group contacted Parks Canada SAR directly. Rescuers were able to heli-sling the group out.

Climbers (blue circle) awaiting rescue at the base of the Rick Blak Memorial Route. A climber fell near the top of the pitch and was moved to an open area to be extracted. *Parks Canada*

ANALYSIS

The climber had placed adequate protection and was reported to be just above her last screw. The party was very experienced, and their VHF radio facilitated a quick rescue with good communications. Moving the patient to a safe open area reduced risk to rescuers. The team had gotten an early start and thus, when the accident happened, it was still early in the day. This gave ample time for the rescue during the short December daylight hours. The accident was a good reminder that all falls on ice can be dangerous and that it is always a good idea to test tool placements and climb well within one's abilities. *(Source: Parks Canada.)*

STRANDED | Bad Weather, Inexperience

Alberta, Jasper National Park, Mt. Athabasca

On May 19, a party of two climbers ascended the north face route (1,500 meters, Grade III) on Mt. Athabasca, reaching the 3,491-meter summit after 13 hours of climbing. During the ascent, one of the climbers was hit by rockfall and sustained minor facial injuries.

At the summit, the climbers were cold, exhausted, and unsure of how to get down in the poor visibility. They sent out an SOS with their ZOLEO satellite communication device, then dug a small hole in the snow and wrapped themselves in a space blanket. Parks Canada SAR made multiple attempts by helicopter to reach them but were unsuccessful due to poor weather. During the last flight, a small weather window allowed rescuers to drop a tent, sleeping bags, food, and a stove for the climbers.

The next morning, the weather prevented helicopter operations. Consequently, two Parks Canada rescuers started climbing the mountain via the Athabasca-Andromeda Col (AA Col). That afternoon, the weather cleared and another set of rescuers was flown to the saddle between Athabasca's summit and the adjacent Silverhorn. Rescuers climbed to the stranded pair and facilitated a helicopter pickup.

The two climbers (yellow circle) hunkered down at the summit of Mt. Athabasca, waiting for a rescue after climbing the north face. Variable weather and the sheer magnitude of alpine climbing in the Canadian Rockies play major roles in annual accidents. ***Parks Canada***

ANALYSIS

Mt. Athabasca is one of the most accessible and popular 11,000-footers in the Rockies. All the routes are heavily glaciated and can be challenging to navigate in poor weather. The north face route has changed dramatically over the years due to melting ice. The final mixed pitch once had plentiful ice and one move graded 5.3; now the lack of ice can bump the grade up to anywhere from 5.7 to 5.10 or M6. The added technical challenge and general fatigue contributed to these climbers' stranding. This was compounded by a lack of experience, poor navigation tools, and absence of familiarity with the descent. *(Source: Parks Canada.)*

AVALANCHE ON APPROACH | Deep Persistent Wind Slab

Alberta, Banff National Park, Crowfoot Peak

On December 15, two climbers set off across Bow Lake to climb C-Train (200 meters, M6), an alpine mixed route on the north face of North Crowfoot Peak. The approach requires ascending a 400-meter snow fan to reach the base of the cliff.

When the two climbers were 300 meters up the fan, they crossed a steep moraine. This released an avalanche above them. One climber jumped off the slab, while the other was carried about 275 meters down the slope. The latter was partially buried and received a large laceration on the head.

The party member who was not caught immediately pressed SOS on an inReach device, then descended the debris to look for their partner. The climber was located on the surface, and after determining the injuries were minor, the pair decided to self-evacuate. They canceled their SOS and returned to their vehicle; the head laceration was treated at a hospital.

ANALYSIS

The avalanche forecast for the region that day was rated moderate, listing deep persistent slab and wind slab problems. It stated, "Areas with a stiffer slab over the

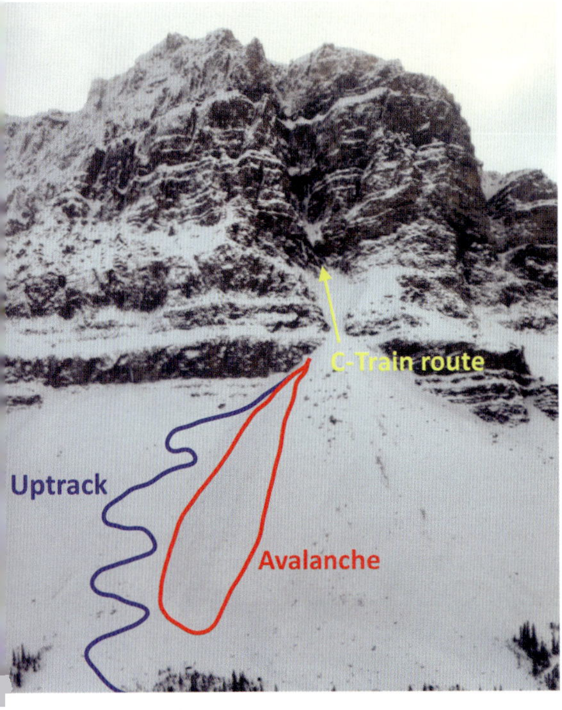

The approach to C-Train on North Crowfoot Peak, showing the climbers' route of ascent in blue and the location of the avalanche in red. ***Parks Canada***

mid-pack facets have the potential to step down to these deeper layers.... the layers have been most reactive in steep, thin, wind-affected spots."

The climbers noticed several "whumphs" and cracking in the snowpack on their way up, which is an indicator of unstable snow. In hindsight, they said, "We should have paid more attention to those, and that we were in the exact kind of terrain the avalanche forecast warned about."

These winter climbers were well prepared for avalanche terrain, wearing transceivers and carrying a shovel and probe each. The upper person was wise to push the SOS button on the inReach immediately, mobilizing rescue resources. They were also smart to cancel their SOS once they realized they could self-evacuate. This is a good example of proper usage of a satellite emergency device. *(Source: Parks Canada.)*

STRANDED | Shoulder Dislocation

Alberta, Banff National Park, Mt. Temple

Early on August 24, Dan Erikson (45) and I, Michael MacLeod (56), started climbing the east ridge of Mt. Temple (1,500 meters, 5.7). We had climbed several times together and are experienced. The weather was cloudy and there was some light precipitation, making the rock slick in places. We initially climbed solo, which is common on this route up to a feature called the Big Step. At that point a rope is used to manage increasing difficulty.

I was climbing up to a ledge several hundred meters below the Big Step. Below, Dan was climbing a short steep section when his foot slipped. The jarring caused by catching himself dislocated his shoulder. The pain was so intense that he couldn't climb. I lowered the rope, set up a haul system, and brought him up to the ledge. I tried to set his shoulder, but the pain was unbearable. It was clear he could not move up or down the mountain.

I gave Dan some painkillers and put an extra jacket on him. We decided the only course of action was to call for a rescue, and we made a cell phone call to Parks Canada. We had an inReach, but using the phone made it easier to coordinate with rescuers.

Steve Holeczi, a Visitor Safety Specialist, and pilot Paul Maloney flew in to scope out the location. They decided on a course of action by factoring in the wind direction, terrain, and other variables. Eventually, they brought Visitor Safety

Specialist Morgen Funston on a long-line and set her down on the ledge beside us. Our packs were flown off first, then the helicopter returned, Morgen attached all three of us to the long-line, and we were lifted off the mountain. A few minutes later, we were at an ambulance at the Moraine Lake parking lot.

For an hour, paramedics tried to set Dan's shoulder without success. At the hospital, the physician explained that the dislocation had crushed the humeral head into the outer socket. This caused the intense pain and the inability to reset the shoulder.

ANALYSIS

This accident is a reminder that things can go wrong unexpectedly and very quickly on a climb, and to be prepared. The slip on the rock appeared minor until Dan realized his shoulder was dislocated. Whether there was a previous weakness in his shoulder is unknown. Having cell service facilitated a rapid response. Packing an inReach as well, along with a first-aid kit, was prudent. *(Source: Michael MacLeod.)*

At the end of 2024, a very experienced climber named Dave Peabody fell to his death while rappelling on the Stanley Headwall (*report below*). The yellow line traces the route, and the blue X marks the spot where the fall took place. *Parks Canada*

RAPPEL FATALITY | Rappel Device Improperly Rigged

British Columbia, Kootenay National Park and Banff National Park, Stanley Headwall

At the end of 2024, a very experienced climber named Dave Peabody (48) fell to his death while rappelling from a route on the Stanley Headwall. Alik Berg was Peabody's partner on that day. He wrote to *ANAC*:

Dave and I had been regular climbing partners for about 12 years with many seasons of winter, alpine, and rock climbing. On December 26 we headed to the Stanley Headwall to climb Drama Queen (170 meters, WI6 M7). This was a fairly routine climbing day for us. That morning we saw teams on French Reality and Dawn of the Dead.

We topped out at dusk (around 5 p.m.) and began rappelling by headlamp. We both used an ATC-Guide on our belay loops and a prusik backup on our leg loops. The last pitch (P4) was the steepest and we climbed on a single rope (blue) with the second rope (red) as a tagline. The pitch was short enough to be rappelled with the blue rope, while red was left fixed at the beginning of the pitch to pull ourselves back in to the anchor atop P3.

This awkward rappel was partly free-hanging, and pulling back in to the belay required care to not disturb a large dripping ice dagger. Dave descended first. I soon joined him. He had already begun setting up the next rappel, threading the red rope through the anchor and joining the two ropes with a single flat overhand knot.

The P3 anchor is a pair of modern bolts with Fixe rap rings. There was enough space on the small ice ledge to not be crowded and we busied ourselves with the routine tasks of rigging the next rappel. I pulled the blue rope, verbally confirming with Dave that the joining knot was in place before making the final tug and pulling up the tail to add a stopper knot. We tied an additional stopper knot in the red rope before tossing it off. We noted that there was a bit of a tangle in the red rope that we'd deal with on the way down.

Dave readied himself to start the rappel. I was distracted with untangling and tossing the remaining rope from the ledge and did not directly observe his connection to the ropes. He started the rappel, moving normally. As Dave descended, my gaze was on the overhand knot joining the rope ends at that moment. I sensed something was off but couldn't register what it was.

At this point, Dave fell. The interval between sensing something was amiss and when Dave started falling was very short, maybe 1 to 2 seconds or less. There was enough time to register this thought but not enough to assess, let alone react. I believe he was about 5 to 10 meters below the anchor when he fell, not when he first stepped off the ledge and weighted the system.

In the immediate aftermath, I became fixated on something being "off" with the knot and that being the likely point of failure. It wasn't until reaching the ground the next morning that it became clear that the knot was not the cause of the accident.

When Dave fell, I reacted by grabbing the free-running (red) rope and squeezing hard enough to melt my gloves and burn my fingers, but not enough to slow his fall. In the darkness I could not see him at the base, only the faint glow of his headlamp. It was about 6 p.m.

The team on French Reality had already left the area. The party on Dawn of the Dead had descended, traversed the base of the wall, and were around the corner and out of earshot. About 15 minutes after the accident, their headlamps reappeared as they looped back into view near the valley bottom—about 1 kilometer northwest of my location. I was able to yell down and they turned around. At 6:45 p.m. they reached the base and we could communicate properly. It was then that they realized the severity of the situation and activated their inReach.

Dave and I had both carried a cell phone and an inReach. I had my cell phone but my inReach was at the base, while Dave had been carrying his on the climb. The party below had enough cell reception to make calls with Garmin dispatch and also Parks Canada.

Parks Canada was able to confirm that I was secure on a solid anchor and a good ledge, and was wearing warm clothing. The rescue team decided that given the exposure and technical nature of the location, they would have to wait until sunrise the following morning to mount a rescue.

During the night I acquired sporadic cell reception and in the morning was able to send a few texts to the rescue team, who suggested delivering ropes to me so I could descend on my own. This was a great idea as it eliminated the risk of doing a direct extrication from the steep wall. At 9:20 a.m. a bag containing two ropes and a radio was delivered to me by helicopter long-line. At 9:50 a.m. I was at the base of the route, where I met rescue team members. *(Sources: Alik Berg and Parks Canada.)*

ANALYSIS

Dave was found with only the blue rope threaded through his device and backup. The device was five to ten meters from the overhand knot.

The matching triple-rated 8.7mm ropes showed no signs of damage, and the joining knot and stopper knots were intact. The stopper knots were unfortunately not photographed, so this comes from the rescuers and my own recollections. However, both parties agreed that the stopper knots were both present.

It appears that Dave's accident was caused by an improperly threaded rappel device. The simple solution to that is a basic partner or function check. Alternately, rappelling using the stacked rappel method is a solution. It is common in guiding practice and deserves broader adoption in the climbing community (*see page 14*).

Though we'll never know exactly what happened here, these are the scenarios that I've come up with:

1. Device and prusik only loaded on blue. During the initial shuffle off the ledge and transition onto steeper ground, both of Dave's hands were gripping the ropes. Once the ropes were fully weighted, Dave transitioned to a looser grip, perhaps one hand, or maybe he released both to deal with a tangled red rope.

2. Same as above, except the red rope snarled the small ice daggers near the end of P3. They supported his body weight on the initial lower-angle terrain while providing similar tactile feedback to a functioning system. Once on steeper ground, his full weight caused the ice to fail or pulled the rope tangle through the constriction that had held it in place.

3. ATC was properly threaded but prusik backup was attached to the blue rope only. When his hands came off braking, the red rope ran free. The stopper knot was not present and the rope tail ran through the ATC. *(Source: Alik Berg.)*

STRANDED | Unable to Climb Out of Canyon

British Columbia, Kootenay National Park, Marble Canyon

On December 17, a group of five climbers decided to climb at Marble Canyon, a popular winter cragging area. All were relatively new to ice climbing. Access to Marble Canyon is somewhat unusual, as climbers must rappel into the canyon and climb out. It is a committing venue despite a short approach and lack of avalanche exposure. There is no walk out. There is also no cell service, and satellite

Marble Canyon is deceptively committing. Though close to the road, free of avalanches, and mostly top-roped, it has no walk-out and poor to non-existent cell/satellite communication. These factors contributed to a group of five requiring a haul-to-the-rim rescue in December 2024. *Parks Canada*

communication devices struggle to function in the deep, narrow canyon.

One of the climbers was more experienced than the others and felt comfortable taking the group to the area. The route chosen was quite difficult (40 meters, WI5). They lowered themselves in and attempted to climb out. The route was in difficult shape, with the bottom barely touching down. Due to the difficulty and their lack of experience, none were able to climb out. Their top-ropes started to freeze in place, making the situation more difficult. Eventually, the more experienced group member was able to ascend a rope using Jumars. This climber initiated an SOS on their inReach.

Parks Canada received the SOS at 4:45 p.m. The initial call created some confusion because the caller provided no details about the nature of the emergency. The SAR team also received two separate iPhone satellite SOS messages from the same area at the same time. None of the stranded climbers responded when asked for more information. By 5 p.m., however, the rescue team had gathered enough information to determine the required response. A team was on scene by 6:30 p.m. They lowered a rescuer and then, one by one, hauled out the four stranded climbers. There were no injuries.

ANALYSIS

This was a group of beginner ice climbers who chose an objective that was too difficult for them. The group had only recently met and they were unfamiliar with each other's experience. After the incident, it was apparent that several members felt uncomfortable descending into the canyon but continued because they felt "it would be okay." It is possible that the most experienced member was overconfident. Yet it is also the responsibility of every climber to speak up when they don't feel comfortable. Know what you are getting into before you go. Some common questions are:

- How difficult is the climbing?
- Is it committing?
- What if we can't do it?
- Who has the communication device and do they know how to use it?
- How do you call for help if needed?
- Do I have the skills to be there? If not, does the group have the skills?
- Do I trust my partners to be responsible for my safety?

Marble Canyon is often in difficult climbing shape. Experienced parties often top-rope routes by lowering in the climber with the belayer at the top. This allows inspection of the route on the way down, and the climber can stop if the bottom isn't formed or looks too difficult. This system also allows for an easy haul system, if necessary.

If you trigger an SOS with a satellite communication device with two-way messaging, please monitor the device. This helps rescuers to respond appropriately and safely. In this case, the climbers were not familiar with their devices and were unaware they had been receiving messages. *(Source: Parks Canada.)*

Brittle and rotten ice contributed to a 50-to-60-foot lead fall on the second pitch of Bourgeau Right (WI4). Note the ice tool (circled red) at the climber's high point. The team self-rescued and then drove eight hours back to Washington state. ***Michael Cariello***

LONG FALL ON ICE

Alberta, Banff National Park, Mt. Bourgeau

On November 23, I (Michael Cariello, 33) went ice climbing with Luke Bracco (21). Our plan was to climb Bourgeau Right (300 meters, WI4). I decided to lead the first pitch, and from the start it was difficult to get good crampon or axe placements, and basketball- to cooler-sized plates were breaking off. Sometimes it would take five or six hits to clear the ice and get a reasonable placement.

I got to a bolt and considered bailing, but because I'd passed the crux and thought it was WI3 to the top, I continued. I got to a ledge at the end of the first pitch, but the bolts were buried under 10 to 20 centimeters of new snow, and I couldn't find them. I knew it was around 50 meters from the base of the climb to the top of the second pitch, so I decided to link the first two pitches. I continued and the ice got really good. Then, with 30 to 40 feet left before the second pitch belay, I got to another crux. At this point, I was out of visual and voice contact with Luke.

I got 10 to 20 feet above my last screw. The ice had become dry and brittle. I was holding on with my left hand and shaking out my right. My ice axe was getting icy from frost (it was 15°F), causing my fingers to begin slipping. It felt like my rubber gloves were making it worse. [*Cariello was wearing Japanese fishermen's gloves, popular among some ice climbers.*] Though they are warm and moisture resistant, these gloves sometimes get a thin buildup of ice, like peanut butter, and glaze over my poles while skiing. This seems to only occur with these gloves. I had never experienced it with ice tools, but on that day I did.

I was being forced to make some fast choices. I didn't trust a screw in the brittle ice, so climbing through the last ten feet felt like the best option. I threw my axe out to the right for the next placement. It took several swings to clear the ice and get it to stick. It wasn't great but felt good enough. When I tried to pull out my left tool, it got stuck. I did a bigger upward pull and my right tool exploded out of the ice. I fell around 50 to 60 feet and either hit something on the way down or partially decked on the belay ledge above the first pitch. I blacked out a bit and realized my right foot was broken. Luke didn't even know I fell.

I lowered and we assessed my foot: The talus was completely shattered and would require six screws, but there was no damage elsewhere. We splinted my foot and, with only four hours until dark, we decided to self-rescue. We did two 60-meter lowers down steep slopes below the climb while I used my good foot to stay upright. Once or twice I swung a bit, had some memorable impacts, and screamed pretty loud. Then I butt-slid a football field length to get to the last anchor. We did another lower, and I crawled from the base of the gully to the parking lot.

ANALYSIS

I made some poor choices to continue in bad conditions and not bail when given the option. A few red flags were the accumulation of new snow (though avalanche danger was moderate) and the unexpected difficulty of the approach. Low morning temperatures were a concern, as they contributed to brittle, poor ice quality. Previous overnight temperatures were between 25° F and 30°F, and on the night before our climb, it dropped to 6°F. *(Source: Michael Cariello.)*

BELAYER HIT BY FALLING ROCK | Loose Rock

Alberta, Banff National Park, Tunnel Mountain

On April 28, a party of two decided to try a new eight-pitch sport route on Tunnel Mountain called The Doe (5.10a). On the fifth or sixth pitch, the leader pulled off a hold and fell. The hold hit the belayer in the head and they momentarily lost consciousness. The belayer was using a Grigri, whose assisted-braking function retained rope control and caught the fall. Eventually, the belayer was able to lower the climber back to the belay. The belayer was bleeding from the head and somewhat confused. The pair did not feel they could descend safely and called for a rescue.

Parks Canada got the call at 3:30 p.m. and responded by helicopter, slightly delayed because the rescue helicopter was busy attending to another rockfall incident elsewhere. Once on scene, the team was able to heli-sling a rescuer to the site and evacuate both climbers.

ANALYSIS

The climbers chose to climb a relatively new route early in the season. Lightly trafficked new routes often have many loose holds, and all routes will have more rubble on ledges and loose rock in the spring due to the freeze-thaw cycle.

The climbers didn't feel comfortable descending after the accident. This was partly due to inexperience and partly because of the injury. Although there are scenarios where a rescue is the safest option, climbers should have the training, experience, and equipment to retreat. Finally, the team did well to employ an assisted-braking belay device. This likely prevented the belayer from losing control of the rope, avoiding a much longer fall for the leader. *(Source: Parks Canada.)*

LEADER FALL | Loose Rock

Alberta, Banff National Park, Mt. Rundle

At 7 p.m. on September 7, a party of two was climbing a multipitch route called Quadra (5.8) on Mt. Rundle. This traditionally protected limestone climb angles up and right on the second and third pitch. On the second pitch, the leader had difficulty with route-finding.

High on the pitch and well above their last protection, the leader dislodged a large block and fell 20 meters. They hit the wall several times and also may have been hit by the falling block. The falling climber was caught by the belayer and was left hanging a significant distance to the right. The leader sustained serious injuries to their back and foot, along with bruises and lacerations; they were unable to either climb or descend. The belayer yelled for help and lowered the leader several meters to a small ledge.

Scene of a leader fall on the route Quadra on Mt. Rundle. The belayer (yellow circle) is in the lower left, and the injured climber (red circle) is above and to the right. A rescuer flown to the scene was able to heli-sling in to the patient, and then both were heli-slung off the mountain. *Parks Canada*

Other climbers heard the rockfall and the belayer's calls for help, and they called Parks Canada Visitor Safety. With limited daylight, the Visitor Safety team flew to the incident, assessed the situation, and staged nearby. A Visitor Safety Specialist was heli-slung to the injured climber on an extended line. They secured the climber to the line, and the two were slung to a waiting ambulance. The belayer was left to rappel and walk down as darkness arrived.

ANALYSIS

This climbing party had enough experience to complete the route. Two factors contributed to the accident. The first was that the route is not commonly climbed and has more loose rock than more popular climbs. Second, the limited availability of protection made for long runouts. These factors, combined with difficult route-finding, led to the long fall and serious injuries. Diligently checking holds and watching for loose blocks is essential in the Canadian Rockies. Thankfully, the gear placed by the leader held, thereby reducing the length of the fall. This probably kept them alive.

The rescue was completed just before dark, thanks to the quick rescue call, precision flying, and there being sufficient rotor clearance to sling a rescuer to the patient. Had the incident occurred a few minutes later or had there been delays in response, a ground-based rescue, taking several hours longer, would have been necessary. Longer responses can result in more complications for the injured. Consider the amount of daylight when choosing an objective—starting early is always a good idea. *(Source: Parks Canada.)*

Pico de Orizaba (18,491 feet), also known as Citlaltépetl, is the third-highest peak in North America. In this view from the northeast, the upper section of the mountain is obscured by storm clouds. These upper reaches saw multiple exposure fatalities in February 2024. *Adam Jones—Wikimedia*

MEXICO

FATAL FALL | Uneven Ropes, No Stopper Knot

Nuevo León, El Potrero Chico

On February 2, Matthew Aaron Richard (27) lost his life in a climbing accident at the Wonder Wall, a popular area behind a swimming pool complex near the canyon's entrance. That evening, a few dozen climbers were barbecuing at the base, and Matt expressed a desire to climb. He and a partner planned to link the first two pitches of the popular Ramsey's Shenanigans (10a) with the last pitch of Evil Shenanigans (10). This entailed three pitches, done as a single 70-meter pitch.

Matt borrowed a new 80-meter rope with a very defined middle mark. He started climbing, with his headlamp illuminating the way. He reached the summit anchors, clipped in direct with his PAS, and yelled down that he would rappel as it had started to rain. He gave the command to take him off belay.

His partner, who was still on the ground, untied and Matt pulled the rope up. From below, even though it was dark, I and others could see Matt setting up a rappel. He started to rappel, cleaning draws. The descent would involve three short rappels. Matt's next set of anchors would have been on a ledge at the top of the second pitch. But we do not know exactly what his plan was.

Around 8:50 p.m., Matt's partner heard something from above and caught sight of Matt's falling body. He yelled, "Charlie, Charlie, call 911!" Those who had medical training rushed over while I contacted emergency services. Matt's friends worked tirelessly to bring him back to life. Rescue volunteers joined the effort but, unfortunately, nothing could be done.

ANALYSIS

Prior to climbing, a friend expressed concern, having earlier seen Matt enjoy an alcoholic beverage. Matt's climbing partner was sober. After some discussion, Matt assured the concerned party and his partner that he had not consumed much alcohol and was feeling very safe to climb. I personally spoke with both climbers to make sure all was safe. I did not witness Matt in a concerning state of inebriation.

After inspection, we found that one end of the rope had a stopper knot and the other did not. The rope was on the ground and undamaged. A single strand was threaded through an ATC-style device in rappel mode. Matt had a third hand backup attached to both his harness and the single rope strand. He had a PAS and a pre-rigged quad (two locking carabiners and one non-locker) clipped to his harness.

Matt's rappel system was not closed. His autoblock backed up the rappel, but would not have prevented him from rappelling off the unknotted end of the rope.

We can assume Matt didn't take note of the middle mark and probably thought he had pulled enough rope through the anchor for both ends to be on the ledge atop the second pitch. It was raining, it was dark, and worse weather was on the way. The anchor stance would have been uncomfortable. He'd have seen his friends having fun below. Any of these factors may have caused him to speed up and make a mistake. *(Source: Charlie Hund. A comprehensive report is available through the ANAC website.)*

EXPOSURE FATALITIES

Puebla, Pico de Orizaba (Citlaltépetl)

On February 17, a group of 12 climbers became stranded in bad weather on Pico de Orizaba (18,491 feet). The group, belonging to a club called Barracracks, had left the trailhead on the southern side of the mountain before being caught in bad weather around 16,700 feet. A cold front had been forecasted, and when it arrived, the mountain was encased in new snow and ice above the 16,000-foot level.

When news that the climbers were missing went out, a search began. Authorities said that the team had not registered, so their climbing plans were unknown. Reports suggest that the group lost their way and became separated.

Helicopters and ground rescuers searched both the south and north sides of the volcano for three days. During that time, five climbers retraced their steps to the original trailhead. One climber managed to reach the northern trailhead after traversing the mountain. Survivors were admitted to the hospital with bruises, hypothermia, and frostbite. Unfortunately, three perished from exposure. These were the group's guide, Luis Flores (57), and climbers José Luis Díaz Morales (57) and Jessica N. (39). Searchers found their bodies during the week following the storm.

ANALYSIS

Pico de Orizaba is a straightforward mountaineering route when in good conditions, but that can quickly change in bad weather. While aware of the forecast, the team may have believed they could summit and descend before the storm arrived. Details are scarce. What is clear is that, despite being technically moderate, this peak presents many hazards. Four people died in a fall on the mountain in August 2023 (*see ANAC 2024*). (*Sources: Explorersweb.com and infobae.com.*)

Italy's Boot on May 7, 2024. A group of skiers is barely visible in the yellow circle. The avalanche runout is marked in red, and the skiers' skin tracks can be seen in the blue rectangles. ***Peter Wojnar***

SKI MOUNTAINEERING

AVALANCHE

Alaska, Denali National Park, Pika Glacier, Italy's Boot

On May 7, a party of five backcountry skiers set out from their base camp on the upper Pika Glacier with the objective of summiting and skiing Italy's Boot (7,510 feet) via its north face. Italy's Boot is a prominent and popular destination on the western edge of the Pika Glacier, as that body of ice flows into the main Kahiltna Glacier. The route required a flat 2.5-mile tour down-glacier to the toe of the face, then a 2,600-foot ascent of the glaciated bowl to the upper summit pitches. Their plan was to ski the route on the descent.

The party left camp at 9:10 a.m. They discussed options when they arrived at the bottom of the climb. The obvious route climbed directly up the face to a high bergschrund. At that point they would decide if proceeding to the summit was feasible. Because of open crevasses along the route, the group stayed roped together.

The team skinned to the bergschrund. The surface snow was powder, sitting atop a stable base. Above the bergschrund the slope became much steeper, and to the climbers' right lay an expanse of blue ice. The party stayed roped up to manage crevasse hazards. They acknowledged that without intermediate protection the rope would provide scant security in the event of a fall.

The snow went from stable to faceted as the team approached exposed rocks near the bottom of the summit pitch. For 200 feet, progress slowed, but after the leader passed the rocks, the climbing became easier and the snow more supportable. The pitch steepened to nearly 50°. Because of the relative ease of travel and the use of an ice axe, Whippet, and crampons by each team member, they placed no protection. Eventually, the leader reached the summit ridge and belayed the rest of the team. The party summited under clear skies at 2:25 p.m. with immaculate views of the Alaska Range.

Upon dropping in, the first skier (Skier 1) decided to ski unroped onto the summit panel, a 400-foot pitch of steep snow. While traversing after his first turn, he triggered a wind slab avalanche. The avalanche broke about six feet above him, knocking him off his feet. He slid 50 feet, but self-arrested on the firm bed surface using a Whippet.

The group lowered a rope to Skier 1. With a belay, he skied the rest of the pitch and built a snow anchor 180 feet down. The remaining four skied or downclimbed to Skier 1 with the safety of a belay. They repeated the process for one more rope length (two of the five skiers elected to sideslip, unroped), until they neared the cliffband above the bergschrund. At that point, the group unroped and skied back to the glacier.

ANALYSIS

The weather over the four days leading up to the incident had been mostly unsettled, with 8 to 16 inches of snow falling in the Pika region. The group noted a mostly right-side-up, stable snowpack in the areas they had traveled. This included terrain of a similar aspect to the Italy's Boot run. They also observed some melt-freeze crusts on solar aspects. They had noted dry loose avalanches on a variety of terrain and wet debris on the Italy's Boot apron during their flight onto the glacier. On the day of the Italy's Boot descent, the weather was clearing, after another seven inches had fallen the previous night.

On May 7, the group made snowpack assessments during the ascent of their intended ski run. They found the majority of the slope to be dry powder sitting atop a stiff snowpack. Above the bergschrund, assessments became more challenging, as the group was roped up with 40 feet between individuals. In hindsight, being roped up exposed the entire group to avalanche hazard—there could have been severe consequences had the avalanche occurred during the ascent. This was the first technical mistake made and, though it ended up as a near miss, it was mere luck that the avalanche did not release.

Starting his descent, Skier 1 dropped in and traversed back to the team's bootpack. There he made the turn that released the slope. Fortunately, Skier 1 was an expert skier and skilled alpinist whose training, instinct, and Whippet likely saved his life as he arrested his fall.

The avalanche ran approximately 2,000 feet of the 2,600-foot ski run. The avalanche was a soft slab, failing on the new snow/old snow interface, specifically running on the bed surface of glacier ice that comprised the skier's left half of the upper pitch. The group believes the ice may have been more reactive than the old snow interface, hence the size and sensitivity of the avalanche. The group classified it as a size D3 (large and destructive) avalanche. Pilots from the local air base

A helicopter photo of the Christian Peak crevasse accident site with rescue personnel visible in the blue rectangle. Note that there is no visible evidence of crevasses, but the accident and later probing revealed multiple thinly bridged slots. Staying roped on glaciers should be a default, not the exception. *Parks Canada*

said they had rarely, if ever, seen this mountain release in such a way.

The second error the group made was not belaying Skier 1 as he dropped in. If Skier 1 had ski cut the slope with a rope on, the slope would have still avalanched but the fall would have been less consequential.

The third, overarching error can be attributed to social factors that have been identified as contributing to avalanche accidents. The group was on the glacier for only one week. They had a list of objectives including Italy's Boot. Thus, summit fever or commitment could have been a key contributing factor. This very experienced party had often skied together, though some members had more mountaineering skills than others. The expert halo may have discouraged some members from speaking up about concerns with the route or travel.

Finally, it has been identified that a four-person party is the optimal size of a group skiing in avalanche terrain. Two is considered the minimum and in parties with more than four people, concerns can be drowned out by others. This can lead parties to be caught in the classic FACETS (Familiarity, Acceptance, Consistency, Expert Halo, Tracks/Scarcity, and Social Facilitation) avalanche heuristic traps. The group size may also have contributed to a communication breakdown.

Once Skier 1 was safely on an anchor, the group did well by staying calm and effecting a safe descent. During the process of self-rescue, the group communicated well, stayed focused, displayed good teamwork, and descended methodically. *(Sources: Skier 1 and the Editors.)*

FATAL CREVASSE FALL | Unroped

Alberta, Banff National Park, Christian Peak

On April 18, an experienced ski touring group was ascending Christian Peak. Also known as Lyell 5 or L5, this is a subpeak of Mt. Lyell, a 3,498-meter peak at the edge of Banff National Park. The ascent was part of a well-traveled traverse of the Lyells.

The group was unroped and traveling in familiar glaciated terrain with good visibility. The depth of the snowpack in the region was reported to be in the range of 150 centimeters to more 300 centimeters, the skies were clear, and the temperature was roughly -20°C with light southwest winds. There were no visible signs of crevasses in the immediate vicinity, and the group was skiing on a track established the day before. There were also extensive ski tracks throughout the area.

The group stopped to reorganize at around 3,200 meters elevation when one of the party members, Rob Coppolillo (54), moved off the track a few meters. He then broke through a thin snow bridge, falling approximately 50 feet into a crevasse.

One of the other group members took charge and immediately initiated a response by contacting a nearby ski touring lodge. The lodge initiated their emergency response plan, and a helicopter with two guides flew to the lodge and picked up two other responders, along with a rope rescue kit, an AED, and medical supplies. They requested a landing area be probed so the helicopter could drop off the rescue group and equipment.

Meanwhile, the members on scene built a T-slot anchor at the top of the crevasse and used a Petzl RAD LINE to rappel to Coppolillo. They found him in a tight constriction, mostly buried by snow. Coppolillo had been traveling uphill and was lightly dressed. Reaching him was difficult because of the amount of digging and squeezing required, and it took roughly an hour after the fall to get to him. The group member who accessed Coppolillo reported no pulse and no breathing, although his airway appeared to be unobstructed.

The four rescuers in the helicopter arrived 45 minutes after the fall. They found a complicated scene. The snowpack was thin (roughly 80 centimeters), and several additional thinly bridged crevasses were identified by probing.

The overall security of the area was in question, as there was almost no visible evidence of Coppolillo's crevasse. The rescue team built several rope systems to safely move around. A rope rescue system was constructed to extract Coppolillo. The group also built a safe landing zone for the evacuation helicopter.

Three rescuers used a 6:1 rope system to raise Coppolillo to the surface after a fourth rescuer descended into the crevasse and attached the line. The fallen skier reached the surface 90 minutes after the fall occurred. CPR began immediately, an AED was applied, and sleeping bags were placed on Coppolillo to reduce heat loss. He was moved to the landing area and Parks Canada Visitor Safety Specialists arrived to transfer him to the rescue helicopter and then on to an air ambulance in Lake Louise at 1:15 p.m. Coppolillo was pronounced deceased at the hospital in Calgary.

ANALYSIS

This experienced group made many appropriate risk management decisions. With the benefit of hindsight, there are several learning points. Roped travel on glaciers, even when there is no evidence of crevasses, should be the default versus the exception. Crevasse hazard can be present even when there are no apparent signs of crevasses despite good visibility. Even when regular probing indicates deep snow, coverage can be highly variable and may be much thinner in some areas. Even the smallest obscure crevasse can be a serious hazard.

Ultralightweight and compact rope systems such as the Petzl RAD LINE can be great tools, but they can be difficult to work with when ropes ice up or loads are high. Pulling on a very thin rope can be difficult. Parties should factor this in when choosing a glacier travel system.

Sometimes when there is an unroped fall into a crevasse, the most difficult part of the rescue is trying to access the clip-in point on the subject's harness. One method to mitigate this issue is to extend the clip-in point to the backpack shoulder by using a sling. This creates a clip-in point in an alternative location.

In a cold environment like during ski season, hypothermia has a rapid onset, and hypothermia can make people more susceptible to a cardiac arrest. One way to reduce the risk of hypothermic cardiac arrest is to handle subjects very gently during resuscitation and evacuation. *(Source: Parks Canada.)*

FALL THROUGH CORNICE | Avalanche

Alberta, Banff National Park, Mt. Temple

On June 20, a party of two were on a ski mountaineering ascent of the southwest ridge of Mt. Temple (3,544 meters). At 9:20 a.m., while climbing the lower section of the ridge (at around 3,350 meters), one of the team members approached too close to the ridgeline and fell through a cornice that overhung the southwest face. A small wind slab (D1.5) was triggered just below the ridge crest, and the subject was carried down through several cliffbands, ending up on lower-angle terrain at approximately 2,700 meters. The subject was not buried.

The subject's partner called Banff National Park by cell phone. After confirming their location, Visitor Safetydispatched a helicopter and rescue team. The climbing partner was advised to attempt to safely locate the subject and provide first aid, or dig them out in the event of a burial.

The southwest face of Mt. Temple. The blue rectangle marks the location of the broken cornice. The red dashed line denotes the path of the falling skier as they were carried by an avalanche over cliffs and steep snow slopes for 650 meters. *Parks Canada*

At 10:15 a.m., the rescue team located the two skiers. The partner was waving at the helicopter to attract attention, while the injured subject was immobile. Two rescuers were slung into the accident site while two other rescuers provided backup in a safe location. Rescuers found the subject alive but seriously injured. They were stabilized and slung to the Lake Louise helipad, where EMS was waiting. The subject was flown directly to Calgary in an air ambulance.

ANALYSIS

The weather and snow conditions on Mt. Temple were conducive to a ski ascent of the chosen route. Both skiers were experienced, and the objective was well within their abilities. They had started early, made good time, and were positioned to be off the mountain by the time conditions deteriorated in the afternoon.

At the time of the accident, the party

was unroped and they were carrying their skis and wearing crampons. They were aware of the cornice but felt they were far enough on the windward side to remain safe. The injured subject does not remember the moment of the accident but said they may have been trying to look over the ridgeline in anticipation of accessing the slope as a ski objective.

This accident reminds us that cornices are notoriously unpredictable. It is difficult to determine where a cornice starts and where safe ground ends. In some cases, cornices collapse farther back than expected, with the fracture line extending onto the ridge itself. The best strategy is to allow a bigger margin than presumed necessary. If terrain forces a skier closer to the ridgeline, consider roping up and moving together. Consider belaying hazardous sections of ridge.

A second learning point is that the party had only one satellite emergency communication device, and it was carried by the person who fell. While this did not become a factor—the emergency call was made by cell phone—a lack of cell service (usually the case in Banff National Park) would have delayed the rescue response. Given the serious injuries, a delay likely would have impacted the outcome. Prudence dictates having more than one satellite communication device in a party. *(Source: Parks Canada.)*

A popular ski tour on Mt. Rainier ends at Camp Muir, a high-altitude refuge at the 10,188-foot level, seen here in the yellow rectangle. Sparse snow led to a falling accident in November 2024. *Walter Siegmund—Wikimedia*

FALL ON SNOW

Washington, Mt. Rainier, Muir Snowfield

I am a 29-year-old female who is new to ski touring. My boyfriend and I were touring to Camp Muir on Mt. Rainier on November 9, 2024. We were familiar with the area, having hiked and done mountaineering there. It was great weather, a little windy, but good visibility. The coverage as we were going up was a mix of ice/snow and rocks since it was early season. We were making great time skinning up and were about halfway up to Camp Miur (10,188 feet) when I lost an edge in an icy section. I tried to catch myself but I couldn't and next thing I knew I was sliding over rocks.

This section happened to be rather steep and with lots of exposed rocks. I wasn't able to self-arrest and at one point I even flipped. It happened so fast that next thing I knew I stopped partway down the slope, a slide of about 50 feet.

I was very fortunate in that aside from bruising my left side (thighs, arm, and ribs), I was fine. We actually continued our ascent for another 20–30 minutes before the adrenaline wore off. I took several ibuprofens and we made the call to turn around and go down.

ANALYSIS

This was one of my first ski tours. Camp Muir is considered a good beginner area as there is minimal avalanche risk and in terms of slope angle, it compares to a blue run. While the early-season conditions and coverage made it more spicy, we were both comfortable up to the point that I fell. I think neither of us realized the hazard or steepness of the slope necessarily until that happened. I think waiting for better snow coverage is probably the way to go for beginner ski tourers.

Reflecting back later, if I had been more injured and unable to ski out on my own, it would have been a very unpleasant experience. I was extremely lucky to not twist or break an ankle falling with my skis attached. It was windy and the cloud cover was coming in so a helicopter might have had trouble landing for a rescue. There were plenty of other skiers on the mountain and several who saw the accident stopped and double-checked that I was okay. We were both prepared and had layers, an emergency bivy, and plenty of food and water. I was wearing a helmet when I fell and was very happy for that, even though I did not hit my head.

The fact that I was new to ski touring could have contributed to the accident. I was also skiing on a brand-new setup that I'd never skied on before, though I don't know if being more experienced with the gear would have prevented the fall. *(Source: Anonymous.)*

FATAL FALL | Low Visibility

Washington, Mt. Rainier, Muir Snowfield

On the afternoon of May 19, National Park Service (NPS) climbing rangers initiated a search for a female skier named Karen Jackmin (38). The initial call for help came from a concerned friend who had last heard from Jackmin a day prior on social media. The post stated the skier was on the Paradise Glacier and embarking on a solo ski tour. Weather on May 18 and 19 at Paradise was overcast with low visibility and snow.

Two NPS rangers were deployed to search Deadhorse Creek Basin, Alta Vista, and the Panorama Face for fresh ski tracks. Another team descended the Muir Snowfield on skis to search the Nisqually and Paradise glaciers, Pebble Creek, and Panorama Point. An additional team of rangers searched the Nisqually River drainage. They all were unable to locate the missing skier.

During a brief weather window on the evening of May 19, rangers aboard the NPS helicopter conducted an aerial search. The rangers located an unresponsive individual in the Nisqually River drainage at the base of Pebble Creek Falls, down in a moat approximately 20 feet deep. The estimated fall distance of 200 feet was deemed not survivable. Building clouds forced the flight's termination. Cell phone data confirmed this individual was likely Jackmin.

Two storm systems delayed recovery, though on May 30, rangers were able to retrieve the ski equipment (one ski and two ski poles) from the top of Pebble Creek Falls. On June 5, the weather had improved and rangers were able to extract Jackmin by an NPS helicopter. On June 12, the commissioner reported that the cause of death was multiple blunt-force injuries consistent with a long fall and ruled the fatality accidental.

ANALYSIS

The Muir Snowfield has been the site of multiple lost climbers or skiers and fatalities. A common theme in most of these incidents is traveling with limited visibility. One technique for traveling in these conditions is to record a GPS track during the ascent to follow during descent. Climbers/skiers also should be aware that clear and sunny conditions can change to clouds and storms within a short time.

Descending the Muir Snowfield is particularly challenging in low visibility as the terrain has a double fall line. Simply following the pull of gravity will likely draw climbers/skiers toward the Nisqually Glacier or toward Pebble Creek. At best, this mistake takes travelers to a crevassed glacier. At worst, climbers/skiers end up on steep terrain exposed to large cliffs.

The latter hazard likely contributed to Jackmin's accident. During recovery efforts, rangers noted that the terrain above Pebble Creek Falls gradually steepens to near vertical. This rollover makes it difficult to see when the slope suddenly drops away. The single ski and two poles found at the rollover point perhaps indicate the skier realized there were cliffs below. She might have been removing her skis in order to climb out of danger when she lost her footing and fell. *(Sources: Mt. Rainier National Park and KOMO News.)*

AVALANCHE

California, Mt. Shasta, Avalanche Gulch

On April 27, two experienced splitboard mountaineers were ascending Avalanche Gulch on Mt. Shasta. The plan was to use this popular route to summit and descend. Around mid-day, they triggered a wind slab avalanche in a feature called the Heart (13,000 feet).

Both people were caught in the avalanche, but neither was buried. Spaced about 20 feet apart, the higher climber (SB 1) arrested his fall near the top of the slab, while the lower climber (SB 2) was carried approximately 1,000 vertical feet downslope. Once the avalanche came to a stop, SB 1 realized he had a knee injury. Nonetheless, he was able to sideslip down to SB 2, who had sustained a broken femur and large puncture and laceration to the lower leg and ribs. Attempts were made to descend but were prevented by intense pain. The pair opted for rescue at 12,200 feet and called 911 at 12:20 p.m.

Siskiyou County SAR, USFS climbing rangers, and the California Highway Patrol (CHP) responded quickly. Conditions for helicopter use were poor due to a whiteout above treeline. Aerial evacuation was attempted, but it was soon clear that ground transport was the only viable option.

The helicopter was able to insert two rescuers to the treeline at about 8,000 feet.

In April 2024, an avalanche was triggered at the top of the Heart feature on Mt. Shasta. It carried a snowboarder 1,000 feet (red arrow) and inflicted a broken femur and other serious injuries. The yellow circle marks the fallen snowboarder. ***Mt. Shasta Climbing Rangers***

After a climb in whiteout conditions, they reached the injured party in several hours. Numerous outfitter mountain guides, who were training on Shasta, also responded up Avalanche Gulch. SB 2 was packaged for a carry-out, and an arduous four-mile evacuation brought the climber down to Bunny Flat trailhead at 6,950 feet.

ANALYSIS

The two splitboarders were skilled mountaineers and very familiar with the terrain. However, the conditions were volatile and challenging. Although there had not been much new snow in the days leading up to the avalanche, strong winds in the upper elevations had blown snow onto the aspect the climbers were ascending.

This wind loading, paired with poor visibility, put the climbers in an unexpected situation, and they did not identify the avalanche hazards before it was too late. When conditions change and visibility diminishes, good observations and decisions become more difficult.

Similarly, with decreased visibility and increased wind, SAR response becomes much more challenging. It was good that the team originally attempted to self-rescue. But following their distress call, the wait was six hours for rescue arrival and six more hours for extraction. When injured and stationary for such an extended interval, frostbite and hypothermia become hazards. While traveling in the alpine, it is imperative to consider the secondary consequences of any accident and pack accordingly. *(Source: Mt. Shasta Climbing Rangers.)*

MULTIPLE AVALANCHES

Utah, Wasatch Mountains, Twin Peaks

On February 11, two parties of backcountry skiers were involved in a serious accident while attempting to summit Twin Peaks (11,330 feet) in the central Wasatch. Group A (a party of three) set off from the Mill B trailhead in Big Cottonwood Canyon at 9 a.m. Their objective was an ascent of Broads Fork to the back of the drainage, gaining the east ridge of Twin Peaks, summiting, and then skiing down the west face.

When Group A arrived in the upper reaches of Broads Fork, they found themselves breaking trail to the back of the basin. As they approached the far wall of the drainage, they realized a solo skier (Skier 1) had been following their track. Skier 1 had begun his approach via the same route, planning to assess conditions on runs lower in Broads Fork. But instead he toured past those runs and followed Group A higher up the canyon.

Center: A climber from Group A near the top of Twin Peaks. Right: Skier 1, barely visible in the red rectangle, is ascending, shortly before being caught and carried in a large slide. *Group A*

Upon reaching upper Broads Fork, Group A focused on their ascent to the ridge. They navigated what they thought to be the most hazardous section: a short pitch of north-facing alpine terrain. With two of the three skiers in a safe spot, the leader broke trail to the ridge. During the ascent, Skier 1 considered chatting with Group A, but never got close enough to talk about their tour and descent plans.

On the ridge, Group A found very sensitive wind slabs on the leeward (south) side of the ridge. They actively mitigated very small wind pillows of snow, noting the hazard. It was then that Skier 1 also gained the ridge. He also noted the wind loading but decided he could manage it. Group A watched Skier 1 leave the ridge and enter the south-facing terrain. Skier 1 skinned down and across the slope on the leeward side below the ridge.

Skier 1 traversed into Lisa Falls, a popular south-facing 5,000-foot run. Upon entering this consequential terrain, Skier 1 triggered a small wind slab, was caught, and was carried for 200 feet. He pulled an airbag, recovered, and tried to quickly descend out of the avalanche path. At this point, Group A lost sight of Skier 1. Out of their sight, another avalanche released above Skier 1, carrying him another 1,000 feet.

After moving farther along the ridge, members of Group A saw that Skier 1 had triggered the larger avalanche and been flushed out of sight. A member of Group A (Skier A) saw a way to access the avalanche's crown and track, thus staying out of hangfire, and then descend the slide path to try to make visual or verbal contact with Skier 1. After a short downclimb and approximately 500 feet of ski descent, they were able to see Skier 1's airbag. Skier 1 was injured and requested help.

Looking up at the debris from the large avalanche that injured Skier 1 in the upper fork of Lisa Falls. The debris field was approximately 1,000 feet long by 350 feet wide, and up to ten feet deep in the gully above. *Group A*

Skier A was able to communicate to his party that he would continue another 500 vertical feet to Skier 1. Group A called 911 from the ridge. Through patchy cell service, Skier A communicated that both he and Skier 1 needed a helicopter rescue. Skier 1 had internal injuries, and Skier A could not safely extricate himself due to the overhead hazard caused by warming and wind loading in extreme terrain. Skier A warmed and packaged Skier 1. They were both hoisted off the mountain by the Utah Department of Public Safety.

ANALYSIS

The avalanche started small but entrained a large volume of snow. By the time it stopped, it was a destructive D2.5 avalanche. Skier 1 was very lucky to survive. He suffered a hemothorax, many broken ribs, and broken facial bones.

The weather and snowpack leading up to the incident were fairly normal for early-to-mid-season Utah. The Wasatch had a lingering persistent weak layer on the northwest through southeast aspects of the compass, at the middle and upper elevations. Beginning on February 1, the range had received 4.5 to 6 feet of snow.

Overnight, the mountains had received another six inches of snow; winds were generally light, with an occasional gust into the 30s along the highest ridgelines. The avalanche hazard was rated considerable on northwest through southeast aspects in the mid- and upper elevations, and moderate elsewhere.

Group A was aware there was a persistent weak layer on much of the north side of the compass. They also knew that south-facing terrain was sunny and wind-loaded. They planned to only travel through one small section of north-facing terrain to access the ridge and then descend a mostly west-facing, windward slope. The skiers in Group A were mountain guides and medical professionals. Their skills played into facilitating the rescue. Though well equipped, they did not have radios, which would have made ridge-to-patient communication easier.

Skier 1 had a more ambiguous travel plan, going into the day with different options. He was excited about the day's clear skies and new snow. Ultimately, this mindset lured him into the upper reaches of Broads Fork and onto Twin Peaks. Then, because of a scarcity or "powder panic" mindset, he decided to drop into sunny and untracked terrain.

If Skier 1 had a strict tour plan matching the forecast, he might have stayed out of harm's way. He may have skied terrain better suited for solo skiing, as well as avoiding the alpine and wind-loaded slopes.

The biggest takeaway is the need for strong communication. Because of the terrain and the pace, an easy opportunity for the two parties to communicate never presented itself. There was never a conversation about respective plans and how those plans might benefit from collaboration versus competition. If an individual arrives to a run and another party is already there, it is the former's responsibility to attempt communication or find a different place to ski.

Extended dry spells followed by big loading events create a dangerous snowpack and dangerous mindsets. Increasingly, we are seeing complex and persistent avalanche problems, along with more people trying to ski fresh snow when storms finally arrive. A growing number of skiers are crowding finite terrain. In these scenarios, planning, patience, and improved communication—both within parties and with others—are ever more important. *(Sources: Skier A, Skier 1, and the Editors.)*

MULTIPLE FALLS | Icy Conditions, Long Sliding Falls

New Hampshire, Mt. Washington, Tuckerman Ravine

At 2:30 p.m. on March 9, a party of two ascended Left Gully with the intention of skiing one of the runs in Tuckerman Ravine. The party traveled on foot across the top of the ravine toward an area above the Lip, a feature near the top of the cirque. At that point, both skiers slipped on the icy surface. They fell approximately 600 vertical feet to the bottom of the ravine, resulting in one fatality (Patient 1, female, 20) and life-threatening injuries to the other (Patient 2).

Mt. Washington Avalanche Center (MWAC) snow rangers and Mt. Washington Volunteer Ski Patrol (MWVSP), along with willing bystanders, effected a rescue and recovery.

Around the same time, a third person (Patient 3) fell from the upper reaches of Hillman's Highway (on an adjacent slope), sustaining critical injuries.

At 2:40 p.m., MWAC and MWVSP rescuers arrived on scene. A helicopter request was denied due to fog and low clouds. Rescuers began the extrication of Patients 1 and 2 in rescue litters down the Tuckerman Ravine Trail. This took one hour and involved two separate teams of rescuers and bystanders who belayed the litters down sections of steep and icy terrain. Patient 2 was eventually transported to Pinkham Notch Visitor Center, where an ambulance was waiting.

At 4 p.m., the rescue team transitioned efforts to Patient 3, and by 6 p.m., Patient 3 was transferred to a snowcat and transported to Pinkham Notch Visitor Center. All rescue efforts were completed by 10 p.m.

ANALYSIS

Recent thawing and refreezing had made Tuckerman Ravine icy and deadly. Over the week prior to the accidents, the Presidential Range saw several days of above-freezing temperatures and rain. This resulted in a loss of 12 inches to the snowpack on the summit of Mt. Washington and at ravine level. Almost two inches of rain fell throughout the week, and on March 6, Mt. Washington Observatory set a high temperature record for the day (40°F).

Temperatures dropped below freezing on March 7, and the snowpack refroze over the next several days. On the day of these accidents, the summit of Mt. Washington recorded an average temperature of 24°F. The snowpack was firm with decreased coverage, exposed rocks, deep holes, and ice throughout Tuckerman Ravine. The avalanche hazard was low, but slide-for-life conditions were very serious.

Dramatic and unpredictable weather on Mt. Washington creates notoriously dangerous conditions. Although hypothermia and avalanches kill many people, the majority of fatalities during the winter are due to long sliding falls. (*See mountwashingtonavalanchecenter.org/danger-zones-mt-washington-by-dougald-macdonald/.*) Here, sliding falls make up 42 percent of fatalities. Prior to March 9, several long, sliding falls occurred that did not result in serious injury.

Conditions impact the ravine differently at different elevations. Soft, edgeable snow at the beginning of an ascent rapidly transitions to firm snow or ice that is impenetrable by ski edges and ice axes. The higher the terrain, the more serious the consequences. *(Sources: Mt. Washington Avalanche Center and the Editors.)*

DATA TABLES

These tables include data from all accidents in the United States and Canada that are reported in this book, plus additional accidents for which data were available. Many climbing accidents each year are not reported. [*For 2024, for example, fewer reports than usual were received from Colorado.*] Therefore, these tables should not be viewed as precise counts of annual climbing accidents, and the data may not represent trends completely accurately. Readers likely will find the most value in the distribution and patterns of accident demographics and causes in Tables II and III.

TABLE I: REPORTED CLIMBING ACCIDENTS*

Year	Accidents Reported		Injured		Fatalities	
	US	CAN	US	CAN	US	CAN
1950s	33	n/a	26	n/a	10	n/a
1960s	66	8	52	7	21	3
1970s	114	18	97	10	34	8
1980s	191	29	124	26	33	8
1990	136	25	125	24	24	4
1991	169	20	147	11	18	6
1992	175	17	144	11	43	6
1993	132	27	121	17	21	1
1994	158	25	131	25	27	5
1995	168	24	134	18	37	7
1996	139	28	100	16	31	6
1997	158	35	148	24	31	13
1998	138	24	138	18	20	1
1999	123	29	91	20	17	10
2000	150	23	121	23	24	7
2001	150	22	138	14	16	2
2002	139	27	105	23	34	6
2003	118	29	105	22	18	6
2004	160	35	140	16	35	14
2005	111	19	85	14	34	7
2006	109	n/a	89	n/a	21	n/a
2007	113	n/a	95	n/a	15	n/a
2008	112	n/a	96	n/a	19	n/a
2009	126	n/a	112	n/a	23	n/a
2010	185	n/a	151	n/a	34	n/a
2011	157	n/a	109	n/a	29	n/a
2012	140	15	121	12	30	2
2013	143	11	100	5	21	4
2014	112	10	89	8	28	1
2015	173	20	111	16	37	4
2016	175	23	134	17	32	6
2017	162	24	116	19	34	2

Year	Accidents Reported		Injured		Fatalities	
	US	CAN	US	CAN	US	CAN
2018	187	17	198	12	17	5
2019	202	18	148	12	31	9
2020	157	19	118	13	28	5
2021	149	11	133	8	28	4
2022	170	22	96	14	40	6
2023	184	31	147	37	51	7
2024	190	20	174	25	49	9
TOTAL	**9,057**	**1,199**	**7,495**	**913**	**1,940**	**356**

* Table I was revised in 2021. The figures presented for the 1950s, 1960s, 1970s, and 1980s are averages of the annual totals for each decade. The category "Total Persons Involved" has been eliminated. The "Total" figures are comprehensive totals from 1951 through 2022. The complete Table I from 1951 to 2019 is archived at publications.americanalpineclub.org.

TABLE II: REPORTED ACCIDENTS BY LOCATION*

Canada*	1959–2023		2024		
Geographic Districts	**Accidents**	**Deaths**	**Accidents**	**Deaths**	**Injured**
Alberta	640	171	10	1	13
British Columbia	385	145	8	8	10
Yukon & Northwest Territories	49	32	1	0	0
Ontario	45	9	2	0	2
Québec	48	10	0	0	0
Eastern Provinces & Territories	9	2	0	0	0

United States*	1951–2023		2024		
Geographic Districts	**Accidents**	**Deaths**	**Accidents**	**Deaths**	**Injured**
Alaska	721	240	5	3	5
Arizona, Nevada, Texas	167	29	7	1	6
Northeast	1362	174	24	3	26
Southeast	335	49	9	0	10
California	1798	378	40	10	34
Central	157	21	0	0	0
Colorado	1178	295	28	11	18
Montana, Idaho, South Dakota	136	52	5	2	3
Oregon	338	146	14	0	16
Utah & New Mexico	315	88	11	2	11
Washington	2134	378	26	11	24
Wyoming	728	177	21	6	21

* The Canada section of Table II was revised in 2021. Eastern Provinces and Territories includes Nunavut, Newfoundland, and the Maritimes. In the U.S., Northeast includes New England and the Mid-Atlantic states (southward to Maryland/Delaware), plus Ohio and Indiana. Southeast includes West Virginia, Virginia, Kentucky, and states farther south. Central incudes Michigan and the Upper Midwest (minus South Dakota), plus Missouri and Arkansas.

TABLE III: ACCIDENT CHARACTERISTICS AND CAUSES

	1951–2023 USA	1959–2023 CAN*	2024 USA	2024 CAN
Terrain				
Rock	6229	661	134	9
Snow	2958	398	40	6
Ice	354	40	8	5
Water	28	3	3	0
Unknown	40	12	5	0
Ascent or Descent				
Ascent	4928	717	86	14
Descent	1790	440	44	2
Unknown[1]	454	24	44	2
Other[1]	99	12	8	3
Climbing Style†				
Alpine/mountaineering	268	30	62	9
Ice and mixed climbing	27	11	7	5
Traditional rock climbing	217	21	49	3
Sport climbing	122	13	32	3
Big-wall climbing	7	0	0	0
Bouldering	26	7	13	0
Top-rope	14	0	0	0
Free solo or DWS	24	3	9	0
Ski mountaineering	37	8	10	3
Other/Not applicable/Unknown	53	6	14	0
Rope Position†				
Leading	241	33	42	4
Seconding	13	0	3	0
Top-roping	12	0	1	1
Roped but not belayed	12	2	3	0
Unroped	224	25	63	6
Rappelling	80	12	15	2
Lowering	31	0	4	0
Belaying	22	6	2	1
Other/Not applicable/Unknown	206	30	83	9

† "Climbing Style" and "Rope Position" categories were introduced in 2021. (The first two columns for each category include data from 2019 to 2023.) "Rope Position" tabulates the position or activity of the person(s) most directly affected by an accident (injured or killed, stranded, near miss, etc.) at the time the incident occurred. "Roped but not belayed" includes simul-climbing and glacier travel. "Unroped" includes bouldering.

	1951–2023 USA	1959–2023 CAN*	2024 USA	2024 CAN
Immediate Causes**				
Fall on rock	4623	374	78	5
Fall on ice (formerly snow or ice)	1285	230	5	2
Fall on snow	56	1	12	1
Falling rock, ice, object	782	164	13	2
Illness[2]	498	28	8	0
Stranded / Lost	516	81	24	7
Avalanche	369	150	7	3
Rappel failure/error[3]	498	66	6	1
Lowering error[4]	62	3	4	0
Fall from anchor	8	1	1	0
Anchor failure	15	1	0	0
Exposure	303	15	4	0
Glissade error	251	18	0	0
Protection pulled out	395	0	1	0
Failure to follow route	262	36	0	0
Fall into crevasse/moat	205	54	1	1
Faulty use of crampons	128	7	0	0
Ascending too fast	93	0	4	0
Skiing[5]	99	20	3	0
Lightning	69	7	0	0
Equipment failure	19	3	0	0
Other[6]	676	45	5	0
Unknown	146	16	30	1
Contributing Causes***				
Climbing unroped	1198	182	18	1
Inexperience	1158	220	2	1
Placed no/inadequate protection	972	117	6	0
Inadequate equipment/clothing	806	79	1	0
Weather	572	84	2	0
Climbing alone	492	75	0	0
No helmet	421	77	2	0
Inadequate belay	339	31	1	0
Protection pulled out (climber placed)	55	8	6	0
Protection pulled out (fixed)	5	0	1	0
Inadequate knot	8	0	2	0
Inadequate backup	20	0	0	0
Rope too short	8	1	0	0
Poor position	301	39	3	0

	1951–2023 USA	1959–2023 CAN*	2024 USA	2024 CAN
Darkness	199	24	0	1
Party separated	149	14	0	0
Loose rock/failure to test holds	205	63	9	2
Off-route	161	24	1	0
Failure to self-arrest	19	0	0	0
Exposure	86	17	4	0
Illness	63	10	3	0
Equipment failure	32	8	0	0
Other[6]	459	125	12	1
Age of Individuals				
Under 15	1259	12	1	1
15–20	1397	209	9	1
21–25	1802	265	22	2
26–30	1701	238	23	3
31–35	2318	23	15	1
36–50	3718	155	39	2
Over 50	573	41	20	3
Unknown	2765	697	89	20
Sex[4]				
Male	1134	120	120	14
Female	333	31	38	2
Not known	265	71	49	18
Experience Level				
Novice	2057	312	1	5
Intermediate	1997	373	0	2
Expert	3001	570	16	17
Unknown	3240	669	84	9
Month				
January	308	30	6	1
February	302	67	10	1
March	461	87	7	0
April	567	54	14	2
May	1192	81	24	2
June	1473	98	19	1
July	2271	290	25	1
August	1342	229	22	5
September	2168	94	13	2
October	618	48	13	0
November	320	26	9	1

	1951–2023 USA	1959–2023 CAN*	2024 USA	2024 CAN
December	167	31	9	4
Unknown	120	4	19	0
Type of Injury/Illness (Data since 1984. Fracture and internal injury breakouts introduced in 2021.)				
Fracture: lower extremity	141	17	27	3
Fracture: upper extremity	21	4	1	0
Fracture: other	45	2	4	0
Spine injury/fracture	46	3	6	0
Total Fractures	*2118*	*291*	*38*	*3*
Laceration	948	96	5	1
Abrasion	499	81	0	0
Bruise	669	92	7	0
Sprain/Strain	550	46	6	0
Head Injury/TBI	491	47	15	1
Internal: chest	11	0	2	0
Internal: abdomen	5	0	1	1
Hypothermia	212	20	17	0
Frostbite	182	14	3	0
Dislocation	199	17	1	1
Puncture	72	14	0	0
Acute mountain sickness	57	0	0	0
HAPE	114	1	0	0
HACE	46	1	0	0
Other[7]	574	72	18	0
None	510	233	12	8

* No Canada data from 2006 to 2011; includes new data from 2012 to 2023.

** "Fall on snow" and "anchor failure" were added in 2021, starting with 2019 data. (Past editions combined falls on snow and ice.) "Protection pulled out" combines two former categories; in this section, the protection pulling out must directly cause the fall. Data from 2022 incidents is missing.

*** Categories introduced in 2021, starting with 2019 data, include "Protection pulled out (climber placed)" and "Protection pulled out (fixed)"; these replaced "Nut/cam pulled out" and "Piton/ice screw pulled out." Other new categories in 2021 were "Inadequate knot," "Inadequate backup," "Rope too short," and "Failure to self-arrest." Data from 2022 incidents is missing.

1 The "Other" category was created in 2001 to reflect that some reported accidents happen when climbers are at the top or bottom of a route, during an approach, or in camp. The category "Unknown" primarily reflects solo climbers.

2 These are illnesses/injuries that led directly or indirectly to an accident or rescue, such as HAPE.

3 Prior years included some lowering errors, anchor failures, and inadequate backups (now their own categories).

4 Categories introduced in 2016.

5 This category covers ski mountaineering. Backcountry ski touring or snowshoeing incidents, including those involving avalanches, are not counted in these tables.

6 These included ice dam collapse, false information on hiking app, and triggered autism.

7 These included amputation, transected bicep muscle, anaphylaxis, and others. Note: Injuries are counted only once in each category for a given incident. For example, an accident that results in two broken ankles will be listed once under "Fracture: lower extremity."